TABLE OF CONTENTS

Introduction 2-3

Daily Warm-Up Lessons 4-123
Five questions for every day

Quizzes 124-135
One quiz for every 10 Warm-Up Lessons

Answer Key 136

INTRODUCTION

Daily Core Curriculum provides your students with five starter activities to capture interest at the beginning of the classroom day or start of a new subject. Each daily activity includes key concepts in the following five core subject areas:

    Language & Grammar
    Geography
    Math
    Science
    Writing

Daily Core Curriculum has been designed for any elementary classroom, regardless of the textbooks or other supplementary programs being used. Implementation of the *Daily Core Curriculum* program is easy. Place the five exercises for the day on the chalkboard, duplicate the questions for students, and/or project them on an overhead projector by photocopying the student pages as transparencies. Another option is to create a flip chart by binding each day's activities at the top. String or a dowel rod can be placed through the binding. Then, the pages can just be flipped each day. You might want to bind the activities one month at a time. Additionally, you can use the appropriate starter in the content area of your classroom's schedule.

There are many other uses for this book. It can be used for those students who finish early or as part of a center. If you are interested in creating more interest, correct answers can be acknowledged each week. Put all the papers in a box or bag, and choose one at random. If the one you have chosen has the correct answer, that student can receive an award or prize.

PROGRAM DESIGN

This book contains daily activities with a starter for both the language and math subject areas. There are 120 lessons, and a quiz is located at the end of the book for every 10 lessons (12 quizzes in all). The quizzes include the questions covered in the lessons in standardized test format. Consider using the quizzes in place of the daily activity.

As a whole, this book contains enough material for you to use for each morning of your school year. The left-hand page is the student page. This page includes two day's worth of lessons, of which you can photocopy, cut in half, and hand out. The right-hand page includes the answers to each question. Here is an explanation of each part of the daily lessons:

Did You Know?

This includes an important fact in one of the following areas: history, geography, science, critters, human body, animals, and feelings. A thought-provoking journal prompt is given that is based on the fact. The journal prompt provides a good starter for transition times — before/after recess, before/after lunchtime, or as a starter to writing time on your schedule. Textbooks and research materials (encyclopedias, almanacs, and even Internet access) may be helpful with some journal prompts.

Language
Daily practice is given in the areas of capitalization, punctuation, spelling, and grammar. This is a good starter for language arts and/or reading time on your schedule.

Math
Students are challenged with daily problems that are aligned with the NCTM *Standards*. This is a good starter for math time on your schedule.

Science
All areas of the science curriculum are covered. This is a good starter for science time on the schedule. Textbooks and research materials (encyclopedias, almanacs, and Internet access) may be helpful with these questions.

Geography
United States and world geography are reviewed as well as map skills and key terms by grade level. This is a good starter for history or social studies time on your schedule. Textbooks and research materials (encyclopedias, almanacs, and Internet access) may be helpful with these questions.

TIME MANAGEMENT
Students quickly become focused as they copy the starters and begin answering them. For some questions, students may need to use textbooks and reference materials to search for answers. Each problem usually takes no more than five to seven minutes to complete. It is recommended (for consistency) that the exercises be used on a daily basis versus once a week.

Enjoy *Daily Core Curriculum* each day of the school year!

Name: _____

LANGUAGE (correct this sentence)
I am in second grade _____

MATH
How much money is one dime?

_____

SCIENCE
True or False: You live in a community.

_____

GEOGRAPHY
What state do you live in?

_____

DID YOU KNOW?
All living things are made up of one or more cells. Imagine that you are the size of a cell. Where would you go? What would you do?

Name: _____

LANGUAGE (correct this sentence)

today is september 2 _____

MATH
Jane and Bill were shopping. Jane bought 7 apples. Bill bought 3 apples. How many apples did they buy in all?

_____

SCIENCE
True or False: The sun is a star.

_____

GEOGRAPHY
If you travel to Paris, what country will you be in?

DID YOU KNOW?
All living things go through cycles of growth. Pick an animal that you like. Describe how it looks as a baby and how it looks as a full-grown adult.

ANSWER KEY

Lesson 1

LANGUAGE (correct this sentence)

I am in second grade   **I am in second grade.**

MATH
How much money is one dime?

10 cents

GEOGRAPHY
What state do you live in?

Answers will vary.

SCIENCE
True or False: You live in a community.

True

DID YOU KNOW?
All living things are made up of one or more cells. Imagine that you are the size of a cell. Where would you go? What would you do?

ANSWER KEY

Lesson 2

LANGUAGE (correct this sentence)

today is september 2   **Today is September 2.**

MATH
Jane and Bill were shopping. Jane bought 7 apples. Bill bought 3 apples. How many apples did they buy in all?

10 apples

GEOGRAPHY
If you travel to Paris, what country will you be in?

France

SCIENCE
True or False: The sun is a star.

True

DID YOU KNOW?
All living things go through cycles of growth. Pick an animal that you like. Describe how it looks as a baby and how it looks as a full-grown adult.

© Learning Resources, Inc.   Daily Core Curriculum

Lesson 3

Name: _____

LANGUAGE (correct this sentence)

i goed to school on tuesday _____

MATH
Ann planted 3 trees. Yolanda planted 5 trees. How many trees did they plant in all?

_____

SCIENCE
List as many types of trees as you can.

_____

GEOGRAPHY
On which continent do you live?

_____

DID YOU KNOW?
Spiders are not insects. Write about why you think a spider is not an insect.

- -

Lesson 4

Name: _____

LANGUAGE (correct this sentence)

there are thirty days in september _____

MATH
How many minutes are in one hour?

_____

SCIENCE
Which season starts in September?

_____

GEOGRAPHY
What is the capital city of your state?

DID YOU KNOW?
A baby frog is a tadpole. It lives in the water. List 10 things you can find in water.

ANSWER KEY

Lesson 3

LANGUAGE (correct this sentence)

I goed to school on tuesday   **I went to school on Tuesday.**

MATH
Ann planted 3 trees. Yolanda planted 5 trees. How many trees did they plant in all?

8 trees

GEOGRAPHY
On which continent do you live?

North America

SCIENCE
List as many types of trees as you can.

Elm, maple, willow, crabapple, etc.

DID YOU KNOW?
Spiders are not insects. Write about why you think a spider is not an insect.

ANSWER KEY

Lesson 4

LANGUAGE (correct this sentence)

there are thirty days in september   **There are thirty days in September.**

MATH
How many minutes are in one hour?

60 minutes

GEOGRAPHY
What is the capital city of your state?

Answers will vary.

SCIENCE
Which season starts in September?

Autumn or Fall

DID YOU KNOW?
A baby frog is a tadpole. It lives in the water. List 10 things you can find in water.

Lesson 5

Name: _____

LANGUAGE (correct this sentence)

me and my friend are gonna get ice cream cones _____

MATH
There were 9 apples. 7 of them had worms. How many apples were without worms?

_____

SCIENCE
Is temperature measured with a compass or a thermometer?

_____

GEOGRAPHY
True or False: An island has water all around it.

_____

DID YOU KNOW?
Pharaohs and kings made up laws long ago. Do you think people need laws? Why or why not?

Lesson 6

Name: _____

LANGUAGE (correct this sentence)

dad and me rakes leaves yesterday _____

MATH
What number has 2 tens and 6 ones?

_____

SCIENCE
If you plant a seed from an apple, what will grow?

_____

GEOGRAPHY
What is the name of the continent where Brazil is located?

_____

DID YOU KNOW?
A good friend is one of the best things in the world. Write about your good friend. What do you like about him or her?

ANSWER KEY

Lesson 5

LANGUAGE (correct this sentence)
me and my friend are gonna get ice cream cones
My friend and I are going to get ice cream cones.

MATH
There were 9 apples. 7 of them had worms. How many apples were without worms?

2 apples

SCIENCE
Is temperature measured with a compass or a thermometer?

Thermometer

GEOGRAPHY
True or False: An island has water all around it.

True

DID YOU KNOW?
Pharaohs and kings made up laws long ago. Do you think people need laws? Why or why not?

ANSWER KEY

Lesson 6

LANGUAGE (correct this sentence)
dad and me rakes leaves yesterday   **Dad and I raked leaves yesterday.**

MATH
What number has 2 tens and 6 ones?

26

SCIENCE
If you plant a seed from an apple, what will grow?

Apple tree

GEOGRAPHY
What is the name of the continent where Brazil is located?

South America

DID YOU KNOW?
A good friend is one of the best things in the world. Write about your good friend. What do you like about him or her?

© Learning Resources, Inc.

Daily Core Curriculum

Lesson 7

LANGUAGE (correct this sentence)

shes sitting down _____

MATH
5 children were playing. 3 left. How many children were still playing?

SCIENCE
True or False: Earth is the only planet.

GEOGRAPHY
What is the capital of the United States of America?

DID YOU KNOW?
The seven continents are Africa, Asia, Europe, Australia, North America, Antartica and South America. What do you think life is like on another continent?

Lesson 8

LANGUAGE (correct this sentence)

how are you feeling today _____

MATH
Which is more time: 3 minutes or 3 hours?

SCIENCE
True or False: You can use a ruler to measure how much liquid is in a cup.

GEOGRAPHY
True or False: Lakes, rivers, and oceans are all bodies of water.

DID YOU KNOW?
Eating healthy foods keeps you strong. Plan a healthy menu for one day of eating. Record it in your journal.

ANSWER KEY

Lesson 7

LANGUAGE (correct this sentence)
shes sitting down   **She is sitting down.**

MATH
children were playing. 3 left. How many
hildren were still playing?

2 children

SCIENCE
True or False: Earth is the only planet.

False

GEOGRAPHY
What is the capital of the United States of America?

Washington, D.C.

DID YOU KNOW?
The seven continents are Africa, Asia, Europe, Australia, North America, Antartica, and South America. What do you think life is like on another continent?

ANSWER KEY

Lesson 8

LANGUAGE (correct this sentence)
how are you feeling today   **How are you feeling today?**

MATH
Which is more time: 3 minutes or 3 hours?

Three hours

SCIENCE
True or False: You can use a ruler to measure how much liquid is in a cup.

False

GEOGRAPHY
True or False: Lakes, rivers, and oceans are all bodies of water.

True

DID YOU KNOW?
Eating healthy foods keeps you strong. Plan a healthy menu for one day of eating. Record it in your journal.

© Learning Resources, Inc.   Daily Core Curriculum

Lesson 9

Name:

LANGUAGE (correct this sentence)
every wednesday we goed to the store _____

MATH
Write down as many addition facts as you can in five minutes.

SCIENCE
True or False: People are one kind of animal.

GEOGRAPHY
What are the four directions found on a map?

DID YOU KNOW?
In the United States and Canada, there are over 100,000 kinds of insects. If you could be an insect, what would you be? Why?

Lesson 10

Name:

LANGUAGE (correct this sentence)
where is joe going _____

MATH
How many tens are in 46?

SCIENCE
What can you recycle from your house?

GEOGRAPHY
True or False: There are seven poles on Earth.

DID YOU KNOW?
Your body is made up of tiny pieces called cells. What would life be like if you were that small? Write about it.

12 Daily Core Curriculum   © Learning Resources, In

ANSWER KEY

Lesson 9

LANGUAGE (correct this sentence)

every wednesday we goed to the store   Every Wednesday we go to the store.

MATH
Write down as many addition facts as you can in five minutes.

Answers will vary.

SCIENCE
True or False: People are one kind of animal.

True

GEOGRAPHY
What are the four directions found on a map?

North, South, East, West

DID YOU KNOW?
In the United States and Canada, there are over 100,000 kinds of insects. If you could be an insect, what would you be? Why?

ANSWER KEY

Lesson 10

LANGUAGE (correct this sentence)

where is joe going   Where is Joe going?

MATH
How many tens are in 46?

4

SCIENCE
What can you recycle from your house?

Almost all nonfood garbage! Answers will vary.

GEOGRAPHY
True or False: There are seven poles on Earth.

False

DID YOU KNOW?
Your body is made up of tiny pieces called cells. What would life be like if you were that small? Write about it.

© Learning Resources, Inc.   Daily Core Curriculum

Lesson 11

LANGUAGE (correct this sentence)
two people is going tonight _____

MATH
What number has 7 tens and 0 ones?

SCIENCE
What does it mean if an animal species is extinct?

GEOGRAPHY
On which continent is Mexico?

DID YOU KNOW?
Bears eat a lot during the fall to help them during the winter. Create one day's meal plan for a bear. What would you include?

Lesson 12

LANGUAGE (correct this sentence)
mom, will you make macaroni and cheese on thursday

MATH
6 dogs are playing. 2 play dead. How many dogs are not playing dead?

SCIENCE
What sense am I using if I listen to birds chirping?

GEOGRAPHY
The two poles are named _____ and _____.

DID YOU KNOW?
Hieroglyphics (HIGH-row-gli-fics) are writings from ancient Egyptians. Write your own alphabet using symbols.

ANSWER KEY

Lesson 11

LANGUAGE (correct this sentence)

Two people is going tonight   **Two people are going tonight.**

MATH
What number has 7 tens and 0 ones?

70

SCIENCE
What does it mean if an animal species is extinct?

There are no more living animals of that species.

GEOGRAPHY
On which continent is Mexico?

North America

DID YOU KNOW?
Bears eat a lot during the fall to help them during the winter. Create one day's meal plan for a bear. What would you include?

ANSWER KEY

Lesson 12

LANGUAGE (correct this sentence)

mom, will you make macaroni and cheese on thursday

Mom, will you make macaroni and cheese on Thursday?

MATH
6 dogs are playing. 2 play dead. How many dogs are not playing dead?

4 dogs

SCIENCE
What sense am I using if I listen to birds chirping?

Sense of hearing

GEOGRAPHY
The two poles are named _____ and _____.

North Pole and South Pole

DID YOU KNOW?
Hieroglyphics (HIGH-row-gli-fics) are writings from ancient Egyptians. Write your own alphabet using symbols.

© Learning Resources, Inc.   Daily Core Curriculum

Lesson 13

Name: _____

LANGUAGE (correct this sentence)

george washington was the first president _____

MATH
Write this amount of money in dollars and cents: 427 pennies

_____

SCIENCE
What is the name of the part of a flower that is under the ground?

_____

GEOGRAPHY
What is the capital of New Mexico?

_____

DID YOU KNOW?
Your teeth are an important part of digestion. What would it feel like to eat without your teeth? Explain in your journal

---

Lesson 14

Name: _____

LANGUAGE (correct this sentence)

where is mine book it was on the table yesterday _____

MATH
Ben and Dave had two dollars. They spent 50 cents. How much money is left?

_____

SCIENCE
What kind of reptiles lived millions of years ago?

_____

GEOGRAPHY
How many equators are on Earth?

_____

DID YOU KNOW?
All insects have six legs. What would you do if you had six legs?

ANSWER KEY

Lesson 13

LANGUAGE (correct this sentence)
george washington was the first president

George Washington was the first president.

MATH
Write this amount of money in dollars and cents: 427 pennies

$4.27

SCIENCE
What is the name of the part of a flower that is under the ground?

A root

GEOGRAPHY
What is the capital of New Mexico?

Santa Fe

DID YOU KNOW?
Your teeth are an important part of digestion. What would it feel like to eat without your teeth? Explain in your journal.

ANSWER KEY

Lesson 14

LANGUAGE (correct this sentence)
where is mine book it was on the table yesterday

Where is my book? It was on the table yesterday.

MATH
Ken and Dave had two dollars. They spent 50 cents. How much money is left?

$1.50

SCIENCE
What kind of reptiles lived millions of years ago?

Dinosaurs

GEOGRAPHY
How many equators are on Earth?

One Equator

DID YOU KNOW?
All insects have six legs. What would you do if you had six legs?

Daily Core Curriculum

☆ Lesson 15

Name: _____

LANGUAGE (correct this sentence)

in my desk, i have pencils erasers and markers

_____

MATH
Finish this pattern:
5, 10, 15, ___, ___, ___, ___

_____

SCIENCE
Plants give off a gas that humans need. Is it oxygen or carbon dioxide?

_____

GEOGRAPHY
How many states are in the United States of America?

_____

DID YOU KNOW?
Laughter is the best medicine. Write your own joke. Include a dog, a cactus, and a bumblebee.

---------- ✂ ----------

☆ Lesson 16

Name: _____

LANGUAGE (correct this sentence)

my teacher say to always put period at the end of sentence

_____

MATH
If my answer is bigger than the numbers in the problem, did I add or subtract?

_____

SCIENCE
What kind of animal is warm-blooded and takes care of its young?

_____

GEOGRAPHY
What continent and country have the same name?

_____

DID YOU KNOW?
The equator divides Earth into two hemispheres: North and South. What do you think life is like in the Southern Hemisphere?

ANSWER KEY

Lesson 15

LANGUAGE (correct this sentence)

n my desk, i have pencils erasers and markers

In my desk, I have pencils, erasers, and markers.

MATH

Finish this pattern:

, 10, 15, ___, ___, ___, ___

20, 25, 30, 35

SCIENCE

Plants give off a gas that humans need. Is it oxygen or carbon dioxide?

Oxygen

GEOGRAPHY

How many states are in the United States of America?

50 states

DID YOU KNOW?

Laughter is the best medicine. Write your own joke. Include a dog, a cactus, and a bumblebee.

ANSWER KEY

Lesson 16

LANGUAGE (correct this sentence)

my teacher say to always put period at the end of sentence

My teacher says to always put a period at the end of a sentence.

MATH

f my answer is bigger than the numbers in the problem, did I add or subtract?

Add

SCIENCE

What kind of animal is warm-blooded and takes care of its young?

Mammal

GEOGRAPHY

What continent and country have the same name?

Australia

DID YOU KNOW?

The equator divides Earth into two hemispheres: North and South. What do you think life is like in the Southern Hemisphere?

© Learning Resources, Inc. Daily Core Curriculum

Lesson 17

Name: _____

LANGUAGE (correct this sentence)
what did jennifer say about the game _____

MATH
Sally started her homework at 4:00. She finished at 5:30. How long did she work on her homework?

_____

SCIENCE
What type of matter is water: liquid, solid, or gas?

_____

GEOGRAPHY
Atlanta is the capital of what state?

_____

DID YOU KNOW?
The brain, heart, and lungs are all organs. Pick one organ and write how you could make sure it is healthy.

Lesson 18

Name: _____

LANGUAGE (correct this sentence)
the dog barked at the neighbor for too hours _____

MATH
How many sides are on an octagon?

_____

SCIENCE
How do bees help plants?

_____

GEOGRAPHY
In what state is the Los Angeles International Airport located?

_____

DID YOU KNOW?
Flowers help make new plants. Write a poem about your favorite flower. Include colors.

ANSWER KEY

Lesson 17

LANGUAGE (correct this sentence)
what did jennifer say about the game   What did Jennifer say about the game?

MATH
Sally started her homework at 4:00. She finished at 5:30. How long did she work on homework?

1-1/2 hours

SCIENCE
What type of matter is water: liquid, solid or gas?

A liquid

GEOGRAPHY
Atlanta is the capital of what state?

Georgia

DID YOU KNOW?
The brain, heart, and lungs are all organs. Pick one organ and write how you could make sure it is healthy.

ANSWER KEY

Lesson 18

LANGUAGE (correct this sentence)
the dog barked at the neighbor for too hours   The dog barked at the neighbor for two hours.

MATH
How many sides are on an octagon?

Eight sides

SCIENCE
How do bees help plants?

They pollinate the flowers.

GEOGRAPHY
In what state is the Los Angeles International Airport located?

California

DID YOU KNOW?
Flowers help make new plants. Write a poem about your favorite flower. Include colors.

© Learning Resources, Inc.   Daily Core Curriculum

Lesson 19

LANGUAGE (correct this sentence)

why is the sky blue asked jamie _____

MATH
How many inches are in one foot?

SCIENCE
When you hold the north poles of two magnets near each other, what will they do to each other?

GEOGRAPHY
Where is Alabama, in the north or the south?

DID YOU KNOW?
Some insects are harmful. Write about one insect and why it is harmful. What would you do to protect yourself from it?

Lesson 20

Name: _____

LANGUAGE (correct this sentence)

dont jump on the chair yelled dad _____

MATH
How many months are in one year?

SCIENCE
What word means a series of events that happen over and over again, in the same order: cycle or continue?

GEOGRAPHY
What is a hemisphere?

DID YOU KNOW?
One organ in your body does not have a job. It is called the appendix. Your other organs have jobs. Pick an organ in your body and write about its job.

ANSWER KEY

Lesson 19

LANGUAGE (correct this sentence)
why is the sky blue asked jamie   "Why is the sky blue?" asked Jamie.

MATH
How many inches are in one foot?

12 inches

SCIENCE
When you hold the north poles of two magnets near each other, what will they do to each other?

They will repel (or push away) from each other.

GEOGRAPHY
Where is Alabama, in the north or the south?

The south

DID YOU KNOW?
Some insects are harmful. Write about one insect and why it is harmful. What would you do to protect yourself from it?

ANSWER KEY

Lesson 20

LANGUAGE (correct this sentence)
dont jump on the chair yelled dad   "Don't jump on the chair!" yelled dad.

MATH
How many months are in one year?

12 months

SCIENCE
What word means a series of events that happen over and over again, in the same order: cycle or continue?

Cycle

GEOGRAPHY
What is a hemisphere?

A hemisphere is half of the Earth.

DID YOU KNOW?
One organ in your body does not have a job. It is called the appendix. Your other organs have jobs. Pick an organ in your body and write about its job.

Lesson 21

Name: _____

LANGUAGE (correct this sentence)
marcia and jan bringed there bikes to school _____

MATH
3 sisters, 3 brothers, and 2 parents are how many people total in the family?

SCIENCE
What type of landform erupts lava?

GEOGRAPHY
In what state is the Grand Canyon?

DID YOU KNOW?
An insect has a skeleton outside of its body while a human has a skeleton inside its body. What would it feel like to have an exoskeleton, or outer skeleton?

Lesson 22

Name: _____

LANGUAGE (correct this sentence)
she will go two there house at 1200 pm _____

MATH
Laurie went on a trip on September 30th. She returned on December 30th. How many months was she gone?

SCIENCE
What do you call moving air?

GEOGRAPHY
Name the five Great Lakes.

DID YOU KNOW?
A female frog lays 1,000 eggs at a time! Write about 1,000 frogs in your classroom. What would that be like?

ANSWER KEY

Lesson 21

LANGUAGE (correct this sentence)

marcia and jan bringed there bikes to school   **Marcia and Jan brought their bikes to school.**

MATH
3 sisters, 3 brothers, and 2 parents are how many people total in the family?

8 people

SCIENCE
What type of landform erupts lava?

A volcano

GEOGRAPHY
In what state is the Grand Canyon?

Arizona

DID YOU KNOW?
An insect has a skeleton outside of its body, while a human has a skeleton inside its body. What would it feel like to have an exoskeleton, or outer skeleton?

ANSWER KEY

Lesson 22

LANGUAGE (correct this sentence)

she will go two there house at 1200 pm   **She will go to their house at 12:00 p.m.**

MATH
Laurie went on a trip on September 30th. She returned on December 30th. How many months was she gone?

3 months

SCIENCE
What do you call moving air?

Wind

GEOGRAPHY
Name the five Great Lakes.

Lake Huron, Lake Ontario, Lake Michigan, Lake Erie, and Lake Superior

DID YOU KNOW?
A female frog lays 1,000 eggs at a time! Write about 1,000 frogs in your classroom. What would that be like?

© Learning Resources, Inc.

Lesson 23

Name: _____

LANGUAGE (correct this sentence)

i goes to italy every july _____

MATH
What is a sphere?

SCIENCE
Rain, snow, hail, and sleet are examples of what?

GEOGRAPHY
On what continent is Italy located?

DID YOU KNOW?
The Chinese invented paper. List three reasons why paper is useful to you.

Lesson 24

Name: _____

LANGUAGE (correct this sentence)

did you find the book by steven kellogg _____

MATH
John has 22 baseball cards. He sells 10. How many are left?

SCIENCE
Name two products made from plants.

GEOGRAPHY
Many years ago, people settled along these bodies of water for transportation and for a water source. What are they?

DID YOU KNOW?
You have more toys when you share. Write about your favorite toy and who you would like to share it with.

26 Daily Core Curriculum   © Learning Resources, In

ANSWER KEY

Lesson 23

LANGUAGE (correct this sentence)
goes to italy every july   **I go to Italy every July.**

MATH
What is a sphere?

A 3-dimensional circle

SCIENCE
Rain, snow, hail, and sleet are examples of what?

Precipitation

GEOGRAPHY
On what continent is Italy located?

Europe

DID YOU KNOW?
The Chinese invented paper. List three reasons why paper is useful to you.

ANSWER KEY

Lesson 24

LANGUAGE (correct this sentence)
did you find the book by steven kellogg   **Did you find the book by Steven Kellogg?**

MATH
John has 22 baseball cards. He sells 10. How many are left?

12 cards

SCIENCE
Name two products made from plants.

Chocolate, coffee, answers will vary.

GEOGRAPHY
Many years ago, people settled along these bodies of water for transportation and for a water source. What are they?

Rivers

DID YOU KNOW?
You have more toys when you share. Write about your favorite toy and who you would like to share it with.

Lesson 25

Name: _____

LANGUAGE (correct this sentence)
its fall, and the leaves are colored orange _____

MATH
What does the Roman numeral V equal?

_____

SCIENCE
True or False: An insect has three body parts.

_____

GEOGRAPHY
Penguins live on this continent.

_____

DID YOU KNOW?
The Nile is the world's longest river. Write about what your travels would be like on the Nile River.

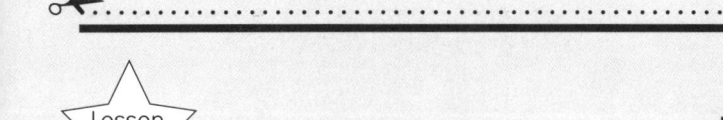

Lesson 26

Name: _____

LANGUAGE (correct this sentence)
i like the song called mary had a little lamb _____

MATH
Are the numbers 3, 7, 9, and 13 even or odd?

_____

SCIENCE
What is it called when animals blend in with their surroundings?

_____

GEOGRAPHY
What is the rugged mountain range that can be found in the western part of the United States?

DID YOU KNOW?
Your mouth, teeth, tongue, stomach, and intestines help you digest your food. Write about a piece of food that goes through your body. What do you think it would see?

ANSWER KEY

Lesson 25

LANGUAGE (correct this sentence)

is fall, and the leaves are colored orange   **It is fall, and the leaves are colored orange.**

MATH
What does the Roman numeral V equal?

5

SCIENCE
True or False: An insect has three body parts.

True

GEOGRAPHY
Penguins live on this continent.

Antarctica

DID YOU KNOW?
The Nile is the world's longest river. Write about what your travels would be like on the Nile River.

ANSWER KEY

Lesson 26

LANGUAGE (correct this sentence)

i like the song called mary had a little lamb   **I like the song called "Mary Had a Little Lamb."**

MATH
Are the numbers 3, 7, 9, and 13 even or odd?

Odd

SCIENCE
What is it called when animals blend in with their surroundings?

Camouflage

GEOGRAPHY
What is the rugged mountain range that can be found in the western part of the United States?

The Rocky Mountains

DID YOU KNOW?
Your mouth, teeth, tongue, stomach, and intestines help you digest your food. Write about a piece of food that goes through your body. What do you think it would see?

Lesson 27

Name: _____

LANGUAGE (correct this sentence)
i went to columbus ohio last august _____

MATH
Which number is bigger: one billion or one trillion?

SCIENCE
What is the source of heat and light for Earth?

GEOGRAPHY
Egypt is located on what continent?

DID YOU KNOW?
To stay healthy, you should drink almost 8 glasses of water each day. When you are thirsty, what do you feel like drinking? Keep a chart of what you drink daily in your journal.

Lesson 28

Name: _____

LANGUAGE (correct this sentence)
gene zion wrote the book harry the dirty dog _____

MATH
Sam collected 7 pounds of apples at the orchard. He made pies with 1 pound. How many pounds were left?

SCIENCE
True or False: There is water inside your body.

GEOGRAPHY
IL is the abbreviation for which state?

DID YOU KNOW?
When a caterpillar changes into a butterfly, it has gone through metamorphosis. Write a story about a caterpillar who has just gone through it. Explain how it feels.

ANSWER KEY

Lesson 27

LANGUAGE (correct this sentence)

went to columbus ohio last august — **I went to Columbus, Ohio last August.**

MATH
Which number is bigger: one billion or one trillion?

One trillion

GEOGRAPHY
Egypt is located on what continent?

Africa

SCIENCE
What is the source of heat and light for Earth?

The Sun

DID YOU KNOW?
To stay healthy, you should drink almost 8 glasses of water each day. When you are thirsty, what do you feel like drinking? Keep a chart of what you drink daily in your journal.

ANSWER KEY

Lesson 28

LANGUAGE (correct this sentence)

gene zion wrote the book harry the dirty dog — **Gene Zion wrote the book Harry the Dirty Dog.**

MATH
Sam collected 7 pounds of apples at the orchard. He made pies with 1 pound. How many pounds were left?

6 pounds

GEOGRAPHY
IL is the abbreviation for which state?

Illinois

SCIENCE
True or False: There is water inside your body.

True

DID YOU KNOW?
When a caterpillar changes into a butterfly, it has gone through metamorphosis. Write a story about a caterpillar who has just gone through it. Explain how it feels.

Lesson 29

Name: _____

LANGUAGE (correct this sentence)
my cat trudy like to eat in the kitchen _____

MATH
The puzzle has 25 pieces. There are 4 corner pieces. How many are not corner pieces?

SCIENCE
What do tadpoles live in?

GEOGRAPHY
NY is the abbreviation for which state?

DID YOU KNOW?
The four seasons are spring, summer, winter, and fall. What is your favorite season? Why?

Lesson 30

Name: _____

LANGUAGE (correct this sentence)
did you go to lunch at 1215 pm or 1230 pm _____

MATH
How many commas belong in the number 1357?

SCIENCE
What is it called when water drops from a cloud?

GEOGRAPHY
How is a map key used?

DID YOU KNOW?
Ladybugs are helpful. They eat the insects that ruin crops. Write a description of a ladybug for someone who has never seen one.

ANSWER KEY

Lesson 29

LANGUAGE (correct this sentence)
ny cat trudy like to eat in the kitchen   My cat Trudy likes to eat in the kitchen.

MATH
The puzzle has 25 pieces. There are 4 corner pieces. How many are not corner pieces?

21 pieces

SCIENCE
What do tadpoles live in?

Water

GEOGRAPHY
NY is the abbreviation for which state?

New York

DID YOU KNOW?
The four seasons are spring, summer, winter, and fall. What is your favorite season? Why?

ANSWER KEY

Lesson 30

LANGUAGE (correct this sentence)
did you go to lunch at 1215 pm or 1230 pm   Did you go to lunch at 12:15 p.m. or 12:30 p.m?

MATH
How many commas belong in the number 1357?

One comma: 1,357

SCIENCE
What is it called when water drops from a cloud?

Rain

GEOGRAPHY
How is a map key used?

A map key is used to label and decode sites on a map.

DID YOU KNOW?
Ladybugs are helpful. They eat the insects that ruin crops. Write a description of a ladybug for someone who has never seen one.

Learning Resources, Inc.   Daily Core Curriculum   33

Lesson 31

LANGUAGE (correct this sentence)

i and susan is going to school today _____

MATH

40 + 20 =

SCIENCE

True or False: All living things need oxygen

GEOGRAPHY

What is the name of the map part that tells directions?

DID YOU KNOW?

A mammal is an animal with fur. List five animals that you think are mammals.

Lesson 32

LANGUAGE (correct this sentence)

the address of the white house is 1600 pennsylvania avenue

MATH

How many millimeters are in one centimeter?

SCIENCE

True or False: Liquids can be changed to solids.

GEOGRAPHY

What do we call the largest bodies of water?

DID YOU KNOW?

The first Olympics were held in Greece over 2,500 years ago. What is your favorite sport to watch during the Olympics? Why?

ANSWER KEY

Lesson 31

LANGUAGE (correct this sentence)

and susan is going to school today   **Susan and I are going to school today.**

MATH

0 + 20 =

60

GEOGRAPHY

What is the name of the map part that tells directions?

Compass

SCIENCE

True or False: All living things need oxygen.

True

DID YOU KNOW?

A mammal is an animal with fur. List five animals that you think are mammals.

ANSWER KEY

Lesson 32

LANGUAGE (correct this sentence)

he address of the white house is 1600 pennsylvania avenue

The address of the White House is 1600 Pennsylvania Avenue.

MATH

How many millimeters are in one centimeter?

10 millimeters in a centimeter

GEOGRAPHY

What do we call the largest bodies of water?

Oceans

SCIENCE

True or False: Liquids can be changed to solids.

True

DID YOU KNOW?

The first Olympics were held in Greece over 2,500 years ago. What is your favorite sport to watch during the Olympics? Why?

Learning Resources, Inc.   Daily Core Curriculum

Lesson 33

Name: _____

LANGUAGE (correct this sentence)
who wants to buy joys dog _____

MATH
Which number is greater: 123 or 321?

_____

SCIENCE
What sense are you using if you use your eyes?

_____

GEOGRAPHY
What is a peninsula?

_____

DID YOU KNOW?
Families can include all kinds of members. What is your family like? What do you like to do with your family?

Lesson 34

Name: _____

LANGUAGE (correct this sentence)
the for brothers are named bill grant jim and ryan _____

MATH
What number is the Roman numeral X?

_____

SCIENCE
How does a whale breathe?

_____

GEOGRAPHY
True or False: There are only four continents in the world.

_____

DID YOU KNOW?
Fertile land is land that is good for growing crops. Write about where you might find fertile land in the world.

ANSWER KEY

Lesson 33

LANGUAGE (correct this sentence)
who wants to buy joys dog   Who wants to buy Joy's dog?

MATH
Which number is greater: 123 or 321?

321

SCIENCE
What sense are you using if you use your eyes?

Sight

GEOGRAPHY
What is a peninsula?

A peninsula is a landform surrounded by water on 3 sides.

DID YOU KNOW?
Families can include all kinds of members. What is your family like? What do you like to do with your family?

ANSWER KEY

Lesson 34

LANGUAGE (correct this sentence)
the for brothers are named bill grant jim and ryan

The four brothers are named Bill, Grant, Jim, and Ryan.

MATH
What number is the Roman numeral X?

10

SCIENCE
How does a whale breathe?

A whale uses its blowhole to breathe.

GEOGRAPHY
True or False: There are only four continents in the world.

False

DID YOU KNOW?
Fertile land is land that is good for growing crops. Write about where you might find fertile land in the world.

Daily Core Curriculum 37

Lesson 35

Name: _____

LANGUAGE (correct this sentence)
stop pushing me shouted gillian _____

MATH
There were 16 ducks. 8 swam away. How many are left?

SCIENCE
True or False: water is a solid.

GEOGRAPHY
Mount McKinley is the tallest mountain in North America. What are mountains made from?

DID YOU KNOW?
To stay healthy, you should follow the Food Guide Pyramid. Think about your lunches at school. How do they fit into the Food Guide Pyramid? In which area do you need to eat more?

Lesson 36

Name: _____

LANGUAGE (correct this sentence)
i likes the song called yankee doodle dandy _____

MATH
Finish the pattern: 2, 4, 8, 16, ___, ___, ___

SCIENCE
True or false: Alligators are reptiles and crocodiles are not.

GEOGRAPHY
What large lake can be found in Utah?

DID YOU KNOW?
When ants live and work together, we call it a colony. Write a story about an ant colony. Include at least 5 different characters in your story.

38 Daily Core Curriculum

ANSWER KEY

Lesson 35

LANGUAGE (correct this sentence)
stop pushing me shouted gillian   "Stop pushing me!" shouted Gillian.

MATH
There were 16 ducks. 8 swam away. How many are left?

8 ducks

SCIENCE
True or False: water is a solid.

False

GEOGRAPHY
Mount McKinley is the tallest mountain in North America. What are mountains made from?

Rock

DID YOU KNOW?
To stay healthy, you should follow the Food Guide Pyramid. Think about your lunches at school. How do they fit into the Food Guide Pyramid? In which area do you need to eat more?

ANSWER KEY

Lesson 36

LANGUAGE (correct this sentence)
i likes the song called yankee doodle dandy   I like the song called "Yankee Doodle Dandy."

MATH
Finish the pattern: 2, 4, 8, 16, ___, ___, ___

32, 64, 128, 256

SCIENCE
True or false: Alligators are reptiles and crocodiles are not.

False

GEOGRAPHY
What large lake can be found in Utah?

Salt Lake

DID YOU KNOW?
When ants live and work together, we call it a colony. Write a story about an ant colony. Include at least 5 different characters in your story.

Lesson 37

LANGUAGE (correct this sentence)

are you going to the jamesons house tonight _____

MATH
How many days are in one year?

_____

SCIENCE
True or False: Earth is the third planet from the sun.

_____

GEOGRAPHY
What is a mountain range?

_____

DID YOU KNOW?
Your blood carries nutrients all around your body. What do you think a blood cell would say if it could talk?

Lesson 38

LANGUAGE (correct this sentence)

henry says it is gonna rain this afternoon _____

MATH
How many sides are there on a pentagon?

_____

SCIENCE
How many legs does an insect have?

_____

GEOGRAPHY
Which one is human-made: An ocean, a building, or a volcano?

_____

DID YOU KNOW?
Water can come in three states of matter: solid (ice), liquid (water), or gas (steam). What happens when you boil water? Draw a picture of what that would look like.

ANSWER KEY

Lesson 37

LANGUAGE (correct this sentence)
are you going to the jamesons house tonight   **Are you going to the Jameson's house tonight?**

MATH
How many days are in one year?

365 days

SCIENCE
True or False: Earth is the third planet from the sun.

True

GEOGRAPHY
What is a mountain range?

A group of mountains

DID YOU KNOW?
Your blood carries nutrients all around your body. What do you think a blood cell would say if it could talk?

ANSWER KEY

Lesson 38

LANGUAGE (correct this sentence)
henry says it is gonna rain this afternoon   **Henry says it's going to rain this afternoon.**

MATH
How many sides are there on a pentagon?

5 sides

SCIENCE
How many legs does an insect have?

6 legs

GEOGRAPHY
Which one is human-made: An ocean, a building, or a volcano?

A building

DID YOU KNOW?
Water can come in three states of matter: solid (ice), liquid (water), or gas (steam). What happens when you boil water? Draw a picture of what that would look like.

Lesson 39

LANGUAGE (correct this sentence)

mr smith went to south carolina on Thursday

MATH
Count by 3s from 0 through 21.

SCIENCE
What is the smallest section of the food pyramid?

GEOGRAPHY
Which state is abbreviated NV?

DID YOU KNOW?
Insects have antennae, or feelers, to feel things. Write a letter to an insect with questions about its antennae.

Lesson 40

LANGUAGE (correct this sentence)

find out how many crayons are in the box

MATH
There are 8 students. How many eyes altogether?

SCIENCE
Where is the sun at noon?

GEOGRAPHY
What direction is between North and West?

DID YOU KNOW?
A turtle is a reptile. Write a story about a turtle that goes to the store. How long would he take and what would he buy?

ANSWER KEY

Lesson 39

LANGUAGE (correct this sentence)

mr smith went to south carolina on Thursday → Mr. Smith went to South Carolina on Thursday.

MATH
Count by 3s from 0 through 21.

3, 6, 9, 12, 15, 18, 21

GEOGRAPHY
Which state is abbreviated NV?

Nevada

SCIENCE
What is the smallest section of the food pyramid?

Fats and sugars

DID YOU KNOW?
Insects have antennae, or feelers, to feel things. Write a letter to an insect with questions about its antennae.

ANSWER KEY

Lesson 40

LANGUAGE (correct this sentence)

find out how many crayons are in the box → Find out how many crayons are in the box.

MATH
There are 8 students. How many eyes altogether?

16 eyes

GEOGRAPHY
What direction is between North and West?

Northwest

SCIENCE
Where is the sun at noon?

At the highest point in the sky, directly overhead

DID YOU KNOW?
A turtle is a reptile. Write a story about a turtle that goes to the store. How long would he take and what would he buy?

Lesson 41 — Mon. — Name:

LANGUAGE (correct this sentence)
my teacher says that i should get my work dun quicker

MATH
What number has 9 hundreds, 6 tens, and 2 ones?

SCIENCE
How many suns are there in our solar system?

GEOGRAPHY
What landform is high, but not as high as a mountain?

DID YOU KNOW?
Tokyo is in Japan. It is a very busy city. Write about a city near you.

Lesson 42 — 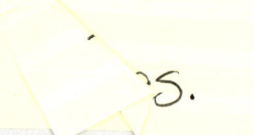 — Name:

LANGUAGE (correct this sentence)
on jan 4, i will go to canada

MATH
How much money is one quarter?

SCIENCE
If a cup of water is left on a shelf for two weeks, what will happen?

GEOGRAPHY
In what state is the Statue of Liberty?

DID YOU KNOW?
You should not eat a lot of sweets. List five snacks that can replace sweets.

ANSWER KEY

Lesson 41

LANGUAGE (correct this sentence)

my teacher says that i should get my work dun quicker

My teacher says that I should get my work done quicker.

MATH
What number has 9 hundreds, 6 tens, and 2 ones?

962

SCIENCE
How many suns are there in our solar system?

One sun

GEOGRAPHY
What landform is high, but not as high as a mountain?

A hill

DID YOU KNOW?
Tokyo is in Japan. It is a very busy city. Write about a city near you.

ANSWER KEY

Lesson 42

LANGUAGE (correct this sentence)

on jan 4, i will go to canada   **On January 4, I will go to Canada.**

MATH
How much money is one quarter?

25 cents

SCIENCE
If a cup of water is left on a shelf for two weeks, what will happen?

The water will evaporate.

GEOGRAPHY
In what state is the Statue of Liberty?

New York

DID YOU KNOW?
You should not eat a lot of sweets. List five snacks that can replace sweets.

Lesson 43 — Weds.

Name: _____

LANGUAGE (correct this sentence)
it is fun when we go to the carnival in oklahoma city
_____

MATH
What number does the Roman numeral III stand for?
_____

SCIENCE
True or False: When you eat, you are using your respiratory system.
_____

GEOGRAPHY
KS is the abbreviation for which state?
_____

DID YOU KNOW?
Rain and snow come from clouds. Write about a trip to a cloud. What would you see there? What could you do?

Lesson 44 — Thurs.

Name: _____

LANGUAGE (correct this sentence)
jodi saw the spider and screamed yikes _____

MATH
Which is greater: five hundred fifty-five or four hundred ninety-nine?
_____

SCIENCE
Sometimes people eat the leaves of plants. Can you think of a plant like that?
_____

GEOGRAPHY
True or False: Lake Superior is north of Lake Michigan.
_____

DID YOU KNOW?
A caterpillar changes into a butterfly. Write about what a day as a butterfly in your backyard would be like.

46 Daily Core Curriculum © Learning Resources, Inc.

ANSWER KEY

Lesson 43

LANGUAGE (correct this sentence)
is fun when we go to the carnival in oklahoma city

It is fun when we go to the carnival in Oklahoma City.

MATH
What number does the Roman numeral III stand for?

3

SCIENCE
True or False: When you eat, you are using your respiratory system.

False

GEOGRAPHY
KS is the abbreviation for which state?

Kansas

DID YOU KNOW?
Rain and snow come from clouds. Write about a trip to a cloud. What would you see there? What could you do?

ANSWER KEY

Lesson 44

LANGUAGE (correct this sentence)
Jodi saw the spider and screamed yikes

Jodi saw the spider and screamed, "Yikes!"

MATH
Which is greater: five hundred fifty-five or four hundred ninety-nine?

five hundred fifty-five

SCIENCE
Sometimes people eat the leaves of plants. Can you think of a plant like that?

Lettuce

GEOGRAPHY
True or False: Lake Superior is north of Lake Michigan.

True

DID YOU KNOW?
A caterpillar changes into a butterfly. Write about what a day as a butterfly in your backyard would be like.

Lesson 45 — Mon.

Name: _____

LANGUAGE (correct this sentence)

i am sposed to eat all of my vegetables _____

MATH
Jennings collected 27 pieces of candy. Then, he got 38 more. How many pieces of candy did he collect in all?

SCIENCE
What two things are needed for a rainbow to form in the sky?

GEOGRAPHY
What is the capital of Japan?

DID YOU KNOW?
Sharks and fish have fins to help them swim. Imagine you are riding on the back of a shark in the ocean. What would you see?

Lesson 46 — Tues.

Name: _____

LANGUAGE (correct this sentence)

me and jacob wants an drink of milk _____

MATH
Write the numeral: forty-seven thousand.

SCIENCE
True or False: Cups can be used to measure solids (like powder) or liquids (like water).

GEOGRAPHY
Is Kansas a city or a state?

DID YOU KNOW?
The Constitution has our most important laws. Write about a law you would like for your class.

Daily Core Curriculum

ANSWER KEY

Lesson 45

LANGUAGE (correct this sentence)
am sposed to eat all of my vegetables   **I am supposed to eat all of my vegetables.**

MATH
ennings collected 27 pieces of candy. Then, e got 38 more. How many pieces of candy id he collect in all?

65 pieces of candy

GEOGRAPHY
What is the capital of Japan?

Tokyo

SCIENCE
What two things are needed for a rainbow to form in the sky?

Rain and sunlight

DID YOU KNOW?
Sharks and fish have fins to help them swim. Imagine you are riding on the back of a shark in the ocean. What would you see?

ANSWER KEY

Lesson 46

LANGUAGE (correct this sentence)
me and jacob wants an drink of milk   **Jacob and I want a drink of milk.**

MATH
Write the numeral: forty-seven thousand.

47,000

GEOGRAPHY
Is Kansas a city or a state?

A state

SCIENCE
True or False: Cups can be used to measure solids (like powder) or liquids (like water).

True

DID YOU KNOW?
The Constitution has our most important laws. Write about a law you would like for your class.

Learning Resources, Inc.   Daily Core Curriculum

 Lesson 47 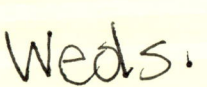 Weds.

Name: _____

LANGUAGE (correct this sentence)

arthur is a character in marc browns books _____

MATH
How much is one nickel worth?

SCIENCE
How many planets are there in our solar system?

GEOGRAPHY
Name one country in South America.

 **DID YOU KNOW?**
A new student can feel very scared. Write a letter for a new student, explaining how you can help at school.

 Lesson 48 Thurs.

Name: _____

LANGUAGE (correct this sentence)

the knicks and the bulls plays a game tomorrow at 700 pm _____

MATH
How many days are in one week?

SCIENCE
True or False: In order to hear sound, there must be air.

GEOGRAPHY
What is TX an abbreviation for?

 **DID YOU KNOW?**
The 13 colonies are 13 states on the East Coast. Write about one of the states in the 13 colonies. What would you find there?

ANSWER KEY

Lesson 47

LANGUAGE (correct this sentence)
arthur is a character in marc browns books   Arthur is a character in Marc Brown's books.

MATH
How much is one nickel worth?

SCIENCE
How many planets are there in our solar system?

5 cents

9 planets

GEOGRAPHY
Name one country in South America.

Brazil, Argentina, Peru, Colombia, Venezuela, Guyana, Suriname, Ecuador, Bolivia, Paraguay, Uruguay, or Chile

DID YOU KNOW?
A new student can feel very scared. Write a letter for a new student, explaining how you can help at school.

ANSWER KEY

Lesson 48

LANGUAGE (correct this sentence)
the knicks and the bulls plays a game tomorrow at 700 pm
The Knicks and the Bulls play a game tomorrow at 7:00 p.m.

MATH
How many days are in one week?

SCIENCE
True or False: In order to hear sound, there must be air.

7 days

True

GEOGRAPHY
What is TX an abbreviation for?

DID YOU KNOW?
The 13 colonies are 13 states on the East Coast. Write about one of the states in the 13 colonies. What would you find there?

Texas

Lesson 49 — Mon.

Name: _____

LANGUAGE (correct this sentence)

nick alice and joey will get trophys for their teamwork

MATH
Write at least 10 math facts that equal 20.

SCIENCE
True or False: When I eat a banana, I am eating a grain.

GEOGRAPHY
Name one state that surrounds Washington, D.C.

DID YOU KNOW?
It is your brain that gives you feelings, not your heart. Write a Valentine poem for you[r] brain.

Lesson 50 — Tues.

Name: _____

LANGUAGE (correct this sentence)

my favorite book is the giving tree by shel silverstein

MATH
Carrie was hopping for 45 minutes. She hopped on her left foot for 20 minutes. How long did she hop on her right foot?

SCIENCE
How many legs do spiders have?

GEOGRAPHY
If I travel from Mexico to Canada, which direction am I traveling?

DID YOU KNOW?
Magnets can attract things made of iron. List three things that you think a magnet could pick up. Try it! Were you right?

ANSWER KEY

Lesson 49

LANGUAGE (correct this sentence)

nick alice and joey will get trophys for their teamwork

Nick, Alice, and Joey will get trophies for their teamwork.

MATH
Write at least 10 math facts that equal 20.

5+15, 25-5, 10+10, 30-10, 1+19, 2+18, 3+17, 28-8, 22-2, 20+0, etc.

SCIENCE
True or False: When I eat a banana, I am eating a grain.

False

GEOGRAPHY
Name one state that surrounds Washington, D.C.

Virginia or Maryland accepted

DID YOU KNOW?
It is your brain that gives you feelings, not your heart. Write a Valentine poem for your brain.

ANSWER KEY

Lesson 50

LANGUAGE (correct this sentence)

my favorite book is the giving tree by shel silverstein

My favorite book is <u>The Giving Tree</u> by Shel Silverstein.

MATH
Carrie was hopping for 45 minutes. She hopped on her left foot for 20 minutes. How long did she hop on her right foot?

25 minutes

SCIENCE
How many legs do spiders have?

8 legs

GEOGRAPHY
If I travel from Mexico to Canada, which direction am I traveling?

North

DID YOU KNOW?
Magnets can attract things made of iron. List three things that you think a magnet could pick up. Try it! Were you right?

Lesson 51 — Weds.   Name: _____

LANGUAGE (correct this sentence)
veterans day is always celebrated on november 11 _____

MATH
What number is the Roman numeral VI?

SCIENCE
True or False: The temperature of any place on Earth depends on what you are wearing.

GEOGRAPHY
The Hudson Bay is surrounded by what country: Canada or Mexico?

DID YOU KNOW?
Thomas Jefferson bought a lot of land in the United States from France. What would you buy if you had a lot of money?

Lesson 52 — Thurs.   Name: _____

LANGUAGE (correct this sentence)
juanita bringed the chips and dip to the party _____

MATH
There were 23 blue corn chips and 65 potato chips. How many chips altogether? Write the equation with your answer.

SCIENCE
What do you call the thick layer of fat that keeps whales warm?

GEOGRAPHY
MT is the abbreviation for what state?

DID YOU KNOW?
Rules are needed for everyone to live together. Write about your least favorite classroom rule. What would you like to change it to?

ANSWER KEY

Lesson 51

LANGUAGE (correct this sentence)
veterans day is always celebrated on november 11
Veteran's Day is always celebrated on November 11.

MATH
What number is the Roman numeral VI?

6

SCIENCE
True or False: The temperature of any place on Earth depends on what you are wearing.

False

GEOGRAPHY
The Hudson Bay is surrounded by what country: Canada or Mexico?

Canada

DID YOU KNOW?
Thomas Jefferson bought a lot of land in the United States from France. What would you buy if you had a lot of money?

ANSWER KEY

Lesson 52

LANGUAGE (correct this sentence)
Juanita bringed the chips and dip to the party   **Juanita brought the chips and dip to the party.**

MATH
There were 23 blue corn chips and 65 potato chips. How many chips altogether? Write the equation with your answer.

23 + 65 = 88 chips altogether

SCIENCE
What do you call the thick layer of fat that keeps whales warm?

Blubber

GEOGRAPHY
MT is the abbreviation for what state?

Montana

DID YOU KNOW?
Rules are needed for everyone to live together. Write about your least favorite classroom rule. What would you like to change it to?

© Learning Resources, Inc.

Lesson 53

Name: _____

LANGUAGE (correct this sentence)
lynnae like going two school _____

MATH
Which is longer: 7 feet or 7 miles?

SCIENCE
The tongue is used for what sense?

GEOGRAPHY
Is Salem a city or a state? Where is it located?

DID YOU KNOW?
The five Great Lakes are Lake Superior, Lake Huron, Lake Michigan, Lake Erie, and Lake Ontario. Write a funny sentence using all the names for the five Great Lakes.

Lesson 54

Name: _____

LANGUAGE (correct this sentence)
the volunteers in are class are vary helpful _____

MATH
Here are fact families for 2, 3, and 5.
2 + 3 = 5, 3 + 2 = 5, 5 − 3 = 2, 5 − 2 = 3
Write two fact families for 3, 4, and 7.

SCIENCE
What things are needed for a seed to grow into a plant?

GEOGRAPHY
What is the name of your county?

DID YOU KNOW?
The taste buds on your tongue help you taste things. Write about an animal that you think does not have taste buds. Explain why.

ANSWER KEY

Lesson 53

LANGUAGE (correct this sentence)
Lynnae like going two school   **Lynnae likes going to school.**

MATH
Which is longer: 7 feet or 7 miles?

7 miles

GEOGRAPHY
Is Salem a city or a state? Where is it located?

Salem is a city in Massachusetts.

SCIENCE
The tongue is used for what sense?

Taste

DID YOU KNOW?
The five Great Lakes are Lake Superior, Lake Huron, Lake Michigan, Lake Erie, and Lake Ontario. Write a funny sentence using all the names for the five Great Lakes.

ANSWER KEY

Lesson 54

LANGUAGE (correct this sentence)
The volunteers in are class are vary helpful   **The volunteers in our class are very helpful.**

MATH
Here are fact families for 2, 3, and 5.
2 + 3 = 5, 3 + 2 = 5, 5 − 3 = 2, 5 − 2 = 3
Write two fact families for 3, 4, and 7.

3 + 4 = 7, 7 - 3 = 4, 7 - 4 = 3, 4 + 3 = 7

GEOGRAPHY
What is the name of your county?

Answers will vary.

SCIENCE
What things are needed for a seed to grow into a plant?

Water, sunlight

DID YOU KNOW?
The taste buds on your tongue help you taste things. Write about an animal that you think does not have taste buds. Explain why.

© Learning Resources, Inc.   Daily Core Curriculum

Lesson 55

LANGUAGE (correct this sentence)
theyre going to the baseball game said lance

MATH
Joeleen was wearing 4 pockets on her pants, 3 pockets on her shirt, and 2 pockets on each shoe. How many pockets in all?

SCIENCE
Sounds are caused by vibrations. What vibrates when you talk?

GEOGRAPHY
True or False: The needle on a compass always points North.

DID YOU KNOW?
A compass needle is a magnet. Explain where you would use a compass and why.

Lesson 56

LANGUAGE (correct this sentence)
the pet dog runned around and around she wus looking for her toy bone

MATH
What number is the Roman numeral II?

SCIENCE
Which is NOT a type of rock: igneous, larvae, sedimentary?

GEOGRAPHY
Name the continent: Paraguay, Argentina, and Ecuador.

DID YOU KNOW?
A group of ants that live together is called an ant colony. Write a letter to your teacher, describing who is in your family.

ANSWER KEY

Lesson 55

LANGUAGE (correct this sentence)

theyre going to the baseball game said lance

"They are going to the baseball game," said Lance.

MATH

Deleen was wearing 4 pockets on her pants, 3 pockets on her shirt, and 2 pockets on each shoe. How many pockets in all?

11 pockets

SCIENCE

Sounds are caused by vibrations. What vibrates when you talk?

Your vocal cords

GEOGRAPHY

True or False: The needle on a compass always points North.

True

DID YOU KNOW?
A compass needle is a magnet. Explain where you would use a compass and why.

ANSWER KEY

Lesson 56

LANGUAGE (correct this sentence)

The pet dog runned around and around she wus looking for her toy bone

The pet dog ran around and around. She was looking for her toy bone.

MATH

What number is the Roman numeral II?

2

SCIENCE

Which is NOT a type of rock: igneous, larvae, sedimentary?

Larvae

GEOGRAPHY

Name the continent: Paraguay, Argentina, and Ecuador.

South America

DID YOU KNOW?
A group of ants that live together is called an ant colony. Write a letter to your teacher, describing who is in your family.

Lesson 57

Name: _____

LANGUAGE (correct this sentence)
how fast can pauline write those letters _____

MATH
What number has 8 tens and 4 ones?

SCIENCE
Knowing that "tri" means three, what do you think Triceratops means?

GEOGRAPHY
What kind of body of water is the Atlantic?

DID YOU KNOW?
Dinosaurs used large tails for balance. What do you think helps you balance? Explain why.

Lesson 58

Name: _____

LANGUAGE (correct this sentence)
mary was born on this day in 1975 how old is she

MATH
Which month has the fewest number of days?

SCIENCE
True or False: All sea animals are fish.

GEOGRAPHY
What state is abbreviated MO?

DID YOU KNOW?
Pioneers moved west on wagons and horses. Imagine you are a pioneer. Write what a day would be like on the trail.

ANSWER KEY

Lesson 57

LANGUAGE (correct this sentence)
ow fast can pauline write those letters   How fast can Pauline write those letters?

MATH
What number has 8 tens and 4 ones?

84

SCIENCE
Knowing that "tri" means three, what do you think Triceratops means?

3-horned dinosaur

GEOGRAPHY
What kind of body of water is the Atlantic?

Ocean

DID YOU KNOW?
Dinosaurs used large tails for balance. What do you think helps you balance? Explain why.

ANSWER KEY

Lesson 58

LANGUAGE (correct this sentence)
mary was born on this day in 1975 how old is she

Mary was born on this day in 1975. How old is she?

MATH
Which month has the fewest number of days?

February, with usually 28 days

SCIENCE
True or False: All sea animals are fish.

False

GEOGRAPHY
What state is abbreviated MO?

Missouri

DID YOU KNOW?
Pioneers moved west on wagons and horses. Imagine you are a pioneer. Write what a day would be like on the trail.

Lesson 59

LANGUAGE (correct this sentence)

on fridays, we go to the restaurant for pizza _____

MATH
Count by tens from 100 to 30.

SCIENCE
Your nose is usually used for what sense?

GEOGRAPHY
What body of water is to the west of Florida?

DID YOU KNOW?
Keeping healthy can make you feel good. List five things that keep you healthy and feeling good.

Lesson 60

LANGUAGE (correct this sentence)

i done it said tony _____

MATH
The centipede walked 100 feet (30.5 m) yesterday and today. if he walked 40 feet (12.2 m) yesterday, how many feet did he walk today?

SCIENCE
True or False: People have traveled to the moon for over 100 years.

GEOGRAPHY
What do you call the section on a map with symbols?

DID YOU KNOW?
People give thanks to their loved ones when celebrating Thanksgiving. Write a letter to your parent(s) explaining how thankful you are.

ANSWER KEY

Lesson 59

LANGUAGE (correct this sentence)

on fridays, we go to the restaurant for pizza   **On Fridays, we go to the restaurant for pizza.**

MATH
Count by tens from 100 to 30.

100, 90, 80, 70, 60, 50, 40, 30

SCIENCE
Your nose is usually used for what sense?

Smell

GEOGRAPHY
What body of water is to the west of Florida?

Gulf of Mexico

DID YOU KNOW?
Keeping healthy can make you feel good. List five things that keep you healthy and feeling good.

ANSWER KEY

Lesson 60

LANGUAGE (correct this sentence)

done it said tony   **"I did it," said Tony.**

MATH
The centipede walked 100 feet (30.5 m) yesterday and today. if he walked 40 feet (12.2 m) yesterday, how many feet did he walk today?

60 feet (18.3m)

SCIENCE
True or False: People have traveled to the moon for over 100 years.

False

GEOGRAPHY
What do you call the section on a map with symbols?

Map key or legend

DID YOU KNOW?
People give thanks to their loved ones when celebrating Thanksgiving. Write a letter to your parent(s) explaining how thankful you are.

Learning Resources, Inc.   Daily Core Curriculum 63

Lesson 61

Name: _____

LANGUAGE (correct this sentence)

what is your favorite dessert _____

MATH
How much money is one penny?

SCIENCE
True or False: Some insects can taste and feel with their antennae.

GEOGRAPHY
What state is an island?

DID YOU KNOW?
Vitamin D helps your teeth and bones grow strong. What would life be like without bones? Write about it.

Lesson 62

Name: _____

LANGUAGE (correct this sentence)

my aunt and uncle live at 845 chance drive _____

MATH
There are 6 pieces of candy. 3 kids want the candy. If the candy is shared equally, how many pieces of candy will each kid get?

SCIENCE
Is the outside crust of the Earth made of rock?

GEOGRAPHY
Which is larger: Cuba or Alaska?

DID YOU KNOW?
Levers are like a wedge that helps you lift something up. Write about what might be under a large rock. What would you find?

64 Daily Core Curriculum © Learning Resources,

ANSWER KEY

Lesson 61

LANGUAGE (correct this sentence)
What is your favorite dessert   **What is your favorite dessert?**

MATH
How much money is one penny?

1 cent

SCIENCE
True or False: Some insects can taste and feel with their antennae.

True

GEOGRAPHY
What state is an island?

Hawaii

DID YOU KNOW?
Vitamin D helps your teeth and bones grow strong. What would life be like without bones? Write about it.

ANSWER KEY

Lesson 62

LANGUAGE (correct this sentence)
my aunt and uncle live at 845 chance drive   **My aunt and uncle live at 845 Chance Drive.**

MATH
There are 6 pieces of candy. 3 kids want the candy. If the candy is shared equally, how many pieces of candy will each kid get?

2 pieces

SCIENCE
Is the outside crust of the Earth made of rock?

Yes

GEOGRAPHY
Which is larger: Cuba or Alaska?

Alaska

DID YOU KNOW?
Levers are like a wedge that helps you lift something up. Write about what might be under a large rock. What would you find?

Learning Resources, Inc.   Daily Core Curriculum 65

Lesson 63

Name:

LANGUAGE (correct this sentence)
december is my favorite month what is yours

MATH
Make 40 cents without a quarter.

SCIENCE
True or False: Magnets attract all types of metal.

GEOGRAPHY
Is South Dakota south of North Dakota?

DID YOU KNOW?
Some dinosaurs ate plants. Plant eaters are called herbivores. Create a dinosaur salad. What would you put in it, and how big would it be?

Lesson 64

Name:

LANGUAGE (correct this sentence)
i seed lions tigers bears and dancers at the circus

MATH
Are these numbers even or odd: 245, 67, 313?

SCIENCE
Does an oak tree make seeds?

GEOGRAPHY
What is Washington, D.C.?

DID YOU KNOW?
States in the south had land for farming called plantations. Would you rather live on a farm or in the city? Why?

ANSWER KEY

Lesson 63

LANGUAGE (correct this sentence)

December is my favorite month what is yours   December is my favorite month. What is yours?

MATH
Make 40 cents without a quarter.

Answers will vary, including 4 dimes, 8 nickels, and 40 pennies.

SCIENCE
True or False: Magnets attract all types of metal.

False

GEOGRAPHY
Is South Dakota south of North Dakota?

Yes

DID YOU KNOW?
Some dinosaurs ate plants. Plant eaters are called herbivores. Create a dinosaur salad. What would you put in it, and how big would it be?

ANSWER KEY

Lesson 64

LANGUAGE (correct this sentence)

i seed lions tigers bears and dancers at the circus

I saw lions, tigers, bears, and dancers at the circus.

MATH
Are these numbers even or odd: 45, 67, 313?

Odd

SCIENCE
Does an oak tree make seeds?

Yes

GEOGRAPHY
What is Washington, D.C.?

The capital of the United States

DID YOU KNOW?
States in the south had land for farming called plantations. Would you rather live on a farm or in the city? Why?

Learning Resources, Inc.   Daily Core Curriculum 67

Lesson 65

LANGUAGE (correct this sentence)
tammy goed on a trip to alabama every december

MATH
Thomas weighs 53 pounds (23.9 kg). Emily weighs 51 pounds (23 kg). What is the sum of Thomas and Emily's weight?

SCIENCE
A duck swims to find its food. A woodpecker looks for insects on trees. Which of these birds needs, webbed feet?

GEOGRAPHY
Does your state border an ocean?

DID YOU KNOW?
It can be embarrassing to fall down. Write about the last embarrassing thing that happened to you.

Lesson 66

LANGUAGE (correct this sentence)
roels birthday is on march 25 2000

MATH
Write 1 dollar and 37 cents in dollars and cents.

SCIENCE
A caterpillar will turn into a _____.

GEOGRAPHY
Name one national park. Where is it?

DID YOU KNOW?
Alaska and Hawaii are the two states that do not touch the rest of the United States. Which state would you rather visit? Explain why.

ANSWER KEY

Lesson 65

LANGUAGE (correct this sentence)
ammy goed on a trip to alabama every december
Tammy goes on a trip to Alabama every December.

MATH
homas weighs 53 pounds (23.9 kg). Emily weighs 51 pounds (23 kg). What is the sum f Thomas and Emily's weight?

104 pounds

SCIENCE
A duck swims to find its food. A woodpecker looks for insects on trees. Which of these birds needs, webbed feet?

A duck needs webbed feet to swim.

GEOGRAPHY
Does your state border an ocean?

Answers will vary.

DID YOU KNOW?
It can be embarrassing to fall down. Write about the last embarrassing thing that happened to you.

ANSWER KEY

Lesson 66

LANGUAGE (correct this sentence)
roels birthday is on march 25 2000   **Raul's birthday is on March 25, 2000.**

MATH
Write 1 dollar and 37 cents in dollars and cents.

$1.37

SCIENCE
A caterpillar will turn into a _____.

Butterfly

GEOGRAPHY
Name one national park. Where is it?

Answers will vary.

DID YOU KNOW?
Alaska and Hawaii are the two states that do not touch the rest of the United States. Which state would you rather visit? Explain why.

© Learning Resources, Inc.

Lesson 67

Name: _____

LANGUAGE (correct this sentence)
aint shelley gonna get her hair cut Today _____

MATH
What time is 20 minutes after 9:15?

_____

SCIENCE
Most plant roots grow in the
_____.

GEOGRAPHY
Name the continent: Canada, Rocky Mountains, Great Lakes.

_____

DID YOU KNOW?
Your heart still beats even when you are sleeping. List five exercises that help your heart.

Lesson 68

Name: _____

LANGUAGE (correct this sentence)
the clock striked midnight it was past elmas bedtime

_____

MATH
Put any needed commas in this number: 76431.

_____

SCIENCE
Matter is anything that has weight and takes up _____.

GEOGRAPHY
True or False: A distance scale is used to show how far away places are from each other.

_____

DID YOU KNOW?
Heat comes from friction. Rub your hands together really fast. Write about how that felt and what your hands felt like after.

ANSWER KEY

Lesson 67

LANGUAGE (correct this sentence)
int shelley gonna get her hair cut Today   **Isn't Shelley going to get her hair cut today?**

MATH
What time is 20 minutes after 9:15?

9:35

SCIENCE
Most plant roots grow in the _____.

Dirt

GEOGRAPHY
Name the continent: Canada, Rocky Mountains, Great Lakes.

North America

DID YOU KNOW?
Your heart still beats even when you are sleeping. List five exercises that help your heart.

ANSWER KEY

Lesson 68

LANGUAGE (correct this sentence)
the clock striked midnight it was past elmas bedtime

The clock struck midnight. It was past Elma's bedtime.

MATH
Put any needed commas in this number: 76431.

76,431

SCIENCE
Matter is anything that has weight and takes up _____.

Space

GEOGRAPHY
True or False: A distance scale is used to show how far away places are from each other.

True

DID YOU KNOW?
Heat comes from friction. Rub your hands together really fast. Write about how that felt and what your hands felt like after.

Learning Resources, Inc.   Daily Core Curriculum

Lesson 69

Name: _____

LANGUAGE (correct this sentence)
L. frank baum wrote the book the wizard of oz _____

MATH
If the year is 2011, and Brandy was born in 2001, how old is she?

SCIENCE
What kind of weather do you like best? Why?

GEOGRAPHY
If I travel to Japan from the United States, I can get there by driving a car. True or False?

DID YOU KNOW?
A fawn is a baby deer. Explain how a baby puppy is like an adult puppy. What is the same? What is different?

Lesson 70

Name: _____

LANGUAGE (correct this sentence)
mom and dad went to the university of iowa _____

MATH
What number is the Roman numeral XII?

SCIENCE
Can sound travel through liquid?

GEOGRAPHY
What is a riverbank?

DID YOU KNOW?
Harriet Tubman helped free slaves on a path called the Underground Railroad. Describe the last time you helped someone.

ANSWER KEY

Lesson 69

LANGUAGE (correct this sentence)
l. frank baum wrote the book the wizard of oz   L. Frank Baum wrote the book <u>The Wizard of Oz.</u>

MATH
If the year is 2011, and Brandy was born in 2001, how old is she?

10 years old

SCIENCE
What kind of weather do you like best? Why?

Answers will vary.

GEOGRAPHY
If I travel to Japan from the United States, I can get there by driving a car. True or False?

False

DID YOU KNOW?
A fawn is a baby deer. Explain how a baby puppy is like an adult puppy. What is the same? What is different?

ANSWER KEY

Lesson 70

LANGUAGE (correct this sentence)
mom and dad went to the university of iowa   Mom and Dad went to the University of Iowa.

MATH
What number is the Roman numeral XII?

12

SCIENCE
Can sound travel through liquid?

Yes

GEOGRAPHY
What is a riverbank?

A riverbank is where the water meets the shore.

DID YOU KNOW?
Harriet Tubman helped free slaves on a path called the Underground Railroad. Describe the last time you helped someone.

Lesson 71

Name: _____

LANGUAGE (correct this sentence)
president bush went to the white house in february

MATH
There were 14 animals in the pet store. 7 were sold. How many pets are in the pet store?

SCIENCE
Erosion is when the surface of the Earth ge[ts] worn down. What can cause erosion?

GEOGRAPHY
What is the abbreviation for Washington?

DID YOU KNOW?
The President of the United States makes decisions for America. Finish this sentence. If I were the president, I would …

Lesson 72

Name: _____

LANGUAGE (correct this sentence)
Who goes with the teacher at 300 pm, is it george or martha

MATH
The table length is 3 feet (.9 m). How many yards is that?

SCIENCE
Seeds can grow without dirt. True or False?

GEOGRAPHY
Is Pennsylvania a city or a state? Locate it on a map.

DID YOU KNOW?
The sun is a star that planets move around. Imagine there was no sun! What would a day be like without sunlight?

ANSWER KEY

Lesson 71

LANGUAGE (correct this sentence)

president bush went to the white house in february

President Bush went to the White House in February.

MATH

There were 14 animals in the pet store. 7 were sold. How many pets are in the pet store?

7 pets

SCIENCE

Erosion is when the surface of the Earth gets worn down. What can cause erosion?

Water, air, and ice

GEOGRAPHY

What is the abbreviation for Washington?

WA

DID YOU KNOW?

The President of the United States makes decisions for America. Finish this sentence: If I were the president, I would …

ANSWER KEY

Lesson 72

LANGUAGE (correct this sentence)

Who goes with the teacher at 300 pm, is it george or martha

Who goes with the teacher at 3:00 p.m.? Is it George or Martha?

MATH

The table length is 3 feet (.9 m). How many yards is that?

1 yard (.9 m)

SCIENCE

Seeds can grow without dirt. True or False?

True

GEOGRAPHY

Is Pennsylvania a city or a state? Locate it on a map.

A state

DID YOU KNOW?

The sun is a star that planets move around. Imagine there was no sun! What would a day be like without sunlight?

Learning Resources, Inc.   Daily Core Curriculum (75)

Lesson 73

Name: _____

LANGUAGE (correct this sentence)
the snowfall maked it hard to drive _____

MATH
What shape is a stop sign?

SCIENCE
Whales are not mammals. True or False?

GEOGRAPHY
Is China a continent or a country?

DID YOU KNOW?
Spiders catch critters in their web to eat. Imagine if you could spin webs the next time you play a sport. How would that help you?

Lesson 74

Name: _____

LANGUAGE (correct this sentence)
i watched many cartoons when i was younger _____

MATH
Can a shape have more than one line of symmetry?

SCIENCE
My town recycles paper. Is a paper towel recyclable?

GEOGRAPHY
If you travel from Maine to Canada, which direction will you be traveling?

DID YOU KNOW?
Your teacher has feelings just like you do. Write a thank you letter to your teacher, for the great job he or she is doing.

ANSWER KEY

Lesson 73

LANGUAGE (correct this sentence)

The snowfall maked it hard to drive   **The snowfall made it hard to drive.**

MATH
What shape is a stop sign?

An octagon

SCIENCE
Whales are not mammals. True or False?

False

GEOGRAPHY
Is China a continent or a country?

A country

DID YOU KNOW?
Spiders catch critters in their web to eat. Imagine if you could spin webs the next time you play a sport. How would that help you?

ANSWER KEY

Lesson 74

LANGUAGE (correct this sentence)

i watched many cartoons when i was younger

I watched many cartoons when I was younger.

MATH
Can a shape have more than one line of symmetry?

Yes

SCIENCE
My town recycles paper. Is a paper towel recyclable?

Yes

GEOGRAPHY
If you travel from Maine to Canada, which direction will you be traveling?

North

DID YOU KNOW?
Your teacher has feelings just like you do. Write a thank you letter to your teacher, for the great job he or she is doing.

Lesson 75

LANGUAGE (correct this sentence)
did amy start at this school in march or april

MATH
Finish the pattern:
11, 22, 33, ____, ____, ____, ____

SCIENCE
Which is NOT used to find out the weather: thermometer, barometer, kilometer?

GEOGRAPHY
What is the postal abbreviation for Colorado?

DID YOU KNOW?
People can look excited. Describe what excited looks like.

Lesson 76

LANGUAGE (correct this sentence)
he ript open the gifts and then he cleaned up the mess

MATH
Write 8 cents in dollar and cents format.

SCIENCE
Where can insects be found?

GEOGRAPHY
What city do you live in?

DID YOU KNOW?
George Washington was the first president of the United States. He is also on the $1 bill. Design a coin or bill with your picture on it. What else would it include?

ANSWER KEY

Lesson 75

LANGUAGE (correct this sentence)

did amy start at this school in march or april   Did Amy start at this school in March or April?

MATH

Finish the pattern:
11, 22, 33, ___, ___, ___, ___

44, 55, 66, 77

SCIENCE

Which is NOT used to find out the weather: thermometer, barometer, kilometer?

Kilometer

GEOGRAPHY

What is the postal abbreviation for Colorado?

CO

DID YOU KNOW?

People can look excited. Describe what excited looks like.

ANSWER KEY

Lesson 76

LANGUAGE (correct this sentence)

he ript open the gifts and then he cleaned up the mess

He ripped open the gifts, and then he cleaned up the mess.

MATH

Write 8 cents in dollar and cents format.

$0.08

SCIENCE

Where can insects be found?

Answers will vary, including in the ground, on trees, flying outside, etc.

GEOGRAPHY

What city do you live in?

Answers will vary.

DID YOU KNOW?

George Washington was the first president of the United States. He is also on the $1 bill. Design a coin or bill with your picture on it. What else would it include?

Learning Resources, Inc.   Daily Core Curriculum

Lesson 77

Name: _____

LANGUAGE (correct this sentence)
what is the abbreviation for street _____

MATH
Write a fact family for 8, 2, and 10.

SCIENCE
Finish this sentence: After lightning, you hear _____.

GEOGRAPHY
Which are larger: ponds or oceans?

DID YOU KNOW?
Earth has a North Pole and a South Pole. Write a letter to a polar bear telling him what you are learning in school today.

Lesson 78

Name: _____

LANGUAGE (correct this sentence)
winter is a good time to go sleding skateing and sking

MATH
Horace had 30 blue balloons, 20 green balloons, and 10 purple balloons. How many balloons did he have altogether?

SCIENCE
What do you use a compass for?

GEOGRAPHY
True or False: The Grand Canyon is in California.

DID YOU KNOW?
A pilgrim is someone who travels to a new land. Finish off this sentence: If I were a pilgrim, I think I would …

80 Daily Core Curriculum

ANSWER KEY

Lesson 77

LANGUAGE (correct this sentence)
what is the abbreviation for street   What is the abbreviation for street?

MATH
Write a fact family for 8, 2, and 10.

$8 + 2 = 10$, $2 + 8 = 10$, $10 - 2 = 8$, $10 - 8 = 2$

SCIENCE
Finish this sentence: After lightning, you hear _____.

Thunder

GEOGRAPHY
Which are larger: ponds or oceans?

Oceans

DID YOU KNOW?
Earth has a North Pole and a South Pole. Write a letter to a polar bear telling him what you are learning in school today.

ANSWER KEY

Lesson 78

LANGUAGE (correct this sentence)
winter is a good time to go sleding skateing and sking
Winter is a good time to go sledding, skating, and skiing.

MATH
Horace had 30 blue balloons, 20 green balloons, and 10 purple balloons. How many balloons did he have altogether?

60 balloons

SCIENCE
What do you use a compass for?

To find the direction you are at

GEOGRAPHY
True or False: The Grand Canyon is in California.

False

DID YOU KNOW?
A pilgrim is someone who travels to a new land. Finish off this sentence: If I were a pilgrim, I think I would …

Learning Resources, Inc.   Daily Core Curriculum

Lesson 79

Name: _____

LANGUAGE (correct this sentence)
Brianna polished her fingernails and her toenails last weds
_____

MATH
Brett bought 22 flowers. He bought 12 flowers with red petals. How many had white petals?
_____

SCIENCE
Why do trees have roots?
_____

GEOGRAPHY
Which state is very small?
_____

DID YOU KNOW?
Your lungs send the oxygen you breathe around your body. Write what it feels like hold your breath.

Lesson 80

Name: _____

LANGUAGE (correct this sentence)
santa said where is rudolph going _____
_____

MATH
Tanisha's dad put her new scooter together. He worked on it for 2 hours on Wednesday. He worked for 3 hours on Friday. On Saturday he finished. He worked 10 hours total. How many hours did Tanisha's dad work on Saturday?
_____

SCIENCE
How much of the earth is covered with water: a.) all b.) about three-fourths c.) about one-half?
_____

GEOGRAPHY
What are continents?
_____

DID YOU KNOW?
A jellyfish does not have a brain. Imagine you are a jellyfish. What would you say?

ANSWER KEY

Lesson 79

LANGUAGE (correct this sentence)

Brianna polished her fingernails and her toenails last weds

Brianna polished her fingernails and toenails last Wednesday.

MATH

Brett bought 22 flowers. He bought 12 flowers with red petals. How many had white petals?

10 flowers

SCIENCE

Why do trees have roots?

To take in nutrients from the soil

GEOGRAPHY

Which state is very small?

Rhode Island

DID YOU KNOW?

Your lungs send the oxygen you breathe in around your body. Write what it feels like to hold your breath.

ANSWER KEY

Lesson 80

LANGUAGE (correct this sentence)

Santa said where is rudolph going   Santa said, "Where is Rudolph going?"

MATH

Tanisha's dad put her new scooter together. He worked on it for 2 hours on Wednesday. He worked for 3 hours on Friday. On Saturday he finished. He worked 10 hours total. How many hours did Tanisha's dad work on Saturday?

5 hours

GEOGRAPHY

What are continents?

Continents are large bodies of land. There are 7 continents on Earth.

SCIENCE

How much of the earth is covered with water: a.) all b.) about three-fourths c.) about one-half?

b.) about three-fourths

DID YOU KNOW?

A jellyfish does not have a brain. Imagine you are a jellyfish. What would you say?

Learning Resources, Inc.   Daily Core Curriculum

Lesson 81

Name: _____

LANGUAGE (correct this sentence)

zach and me is going out to lunch tomorrow _____

MATH
Count by 5s from 35 through 65.

_____

SCIENCE
True or False: Dolphins speak to each other with clicks and whistles.

_____

GEOGRAPHY
What is the country touching Portugal?

_____

DID YOU KNOW?
You have to work very hard to earn something you want. Describe a business you would like to open. What would you sell?

Lesson 82

Name: _____

LANGUAGE (correct this sentence)

winter lasts thru december january february and march

_____

MATH
What number has 4 tens, 6 ones, and 8 hundreds?

_____

SCIENCE
True or False: All living things need water

_____

GEOGRAPHY
Is Boston a city or state?

DID YOU KNOW?
The Pony Express was used a long time ago to carry mail out west. Imagine if you could only send people mail that way. Would you write as much? Explain why.

ANSWER KEY

Lesson 81

LANGUAGE (correct this sentence)

ach and me is going out to lunch tomorrow   Zach and I are going out to lunch tomorrow.

MATH

ount by 5s from 35 through 65.

SCIENCE

True or False: Dolphins speak to each other with clicks and whistles.

5, 40, 45, 50, 55, 60, 65

True

GEOGRAPHY

hat is the country touching Portugal?

DID YOU KNOW?

You have to work very hard to earn something you want. Describe a business you would like to open. What would you sell?

pain

ANSWER KEY

Lesson 82

LANGUAGE (correct this sentence)

winter lasts thru december january february and march

Winter lasts through December, January, February, and March.

MATH

hat number has 4 tens, 6 ones, and 8 undreds?

SCIENCE

True or False: All living things need water.

346

True

GEOGRAPHY

Boston a city or state?

DID YOU KNOW?

The Pony Express was used a long time ago to carry mail out west. Imagine if you could only send people mail that way. Would you write as much? Explain why.

A state

Learning Resources, Inc.   Daily Core Curriculum 85

Lesson 83

Name: _____

LANGUAGE (correct this sentence)

thisll bee the last time i correct sentences this year
_____

MATH
How much is the Roman numeral III?

SCIENCE
True or False: Most plants make their own food.

GEOGRAPHY
Which direction do you travel if you go from California to Oregon?

DID YOU KNOW?
People look at maps to find places, roads and features. Pick a place on a map and write about what you can find there.

Lesson 84

Name: _____

LANGUAGE (correct this sentence)

what day of the week comes after thurs _____

MATH
Write the numbers from largest to smallest: 123, 564, 103, 524.

SCIENCE
Can plants grow in wet and dry places?

GEOGRAPHY
In your address, which two things need a comma between them?

DID YOU KNOW?
The measurement of a foot used to be a king's foot. Come up with something you could use to measure three things in the room. Then try it!

ANSWER KEY

Lesson 83

LANGUAGE (correct this sentence)

thisll bee the last time i correct sentences this year

This will be the last time I correct sentences this year.

MATH

How much is the Roman numeral III?

3

SCIENCE

True or False: Most plants make their own food.

True

GEOGRAPHY

Which direction do you travel if you go from California to Oregon?

North

DID YOU KNOW?

People look at maps to find places, roads, and features. Pick a place on a map and write about what you can find there.

ANSWER KEY

Lesson 84

LANGUAGE (correct this sentence)

what day of the week comes after thurs

What day of the week comes after Thursday?

MATH

Write the numbers from largest to smallest: 123, 564, 103, 524.

564, 524, 123, 103

SCIENCE

Can plants grow in wet and dry places?

Yes

GEOGRAPHY

In your address, which two things need a comma between them?

City, state

DID YOU KNOW?

The measurement of a foot used to be a king's foot. Come up with something you could use to measure three things in the room. Then try it!

Lesson 85

Name: _____

LANGUAGE (correct this sentence)
benjamin is gonna be an artist when he grows up

_____

MATH
List at least 10 math facts that equal 8.

SCIENCE
Which type of measurement is usually used for the temperature outside: Celsius or Fahrenheit?

GEOGRAPHY
On what continent is India?

DID YOU KNOW?

Turtles, lizards, snakes, and alligators are all reptiles. Pick one reptile. Write what you would like to know about that reptile.

- -

Lesson 86

Name: _____

LANGUAGE (correct this sentence)
the class votes for a new president tomarrow

MATH
What number is Roman numeral XI?

SCIENCE
What type of rocks are formed when magma from inside the Earth cools and hardens: a.) sedimentary b.) igneous c.) metamorphic?

GEOGRAPHY
True or False: The Dominican Republic is an island.

DID YOU KNOW?

Icicles form during the winter. Describe how you think they form.

88 Daily Core Curriculum

ANSWER KEY

Lesson 85

LANGUAGE (correct this sentence)

Benjamin is gonna be an artist when he grows up

Benjamin is going to be an artist when he grows up.

MATH
List at least 10 math facts that equal 8.

4 + 4, 2 + 2 + 2, 10 - 2, etc.

SCIENCE
Which type of measurement is usually used for the temperature outside: Celsius or Fahrenheit?

Fahrenheit

GEOGRAPHY
On what continent is India?

Asia

DID YOU KNOW?
Turtles, lizards, snakes, and alligators are all reptiles. Pick one reptile. Write what you would like to know about that reptile.

ANSWER KEY

Lesson 86

LANGUAGE (correct this sentence)

The class votes for a new president tomarrow

The class votes for a new president tomorrow.

MATH
What number is Roman numeral XI?

11

SCIENCE
What type of rocks are formed when magma from inside the Earth cools and hardens: a.) sedimentary b.) igneous c.) metamorphic?

b.) igneous

GEOGRAPHY
True or False: The Dominican Republic is an island.

True

DID YOU KNOW?
Icicles form during the winter. Describe how you think they form.

Lesson 87

LANGUAGE (correct this sentence)
the book im reading now is called click clack moo

MATH
Show 71 cents with 6 coins.

SCIENCE
True or False: The reason why the sun sets and rises is because the sun moves around the Earth.

GEOGRAPHY
What is it called when a product is made in one country and sent to another country: imported or exported?

DID YOU KNOW?
Plants grow from seeds. Write a poem about a plant that grows from a very small seed.

Lesson 88

LANGUAGE (correct this sentence)
mrs johnsons birthday is today she is very young

MATH
How many days are in the month of January?

SCIENCE
Can plants grow in both hot and cold places?

GEOGRAPHY
What state does OK stand for?

DID YOU KNOW?
Sometimes advice helps. Write advice for someone who had a fight with his or her best friend. Try to help the friends make up.

ANSWER KEY

LANGUAGE (correct this sentence)

the book im reading now is called click clack moo

The book I'm reading now is called <u>Click Clack Moo</u>.

MATH

Show 71 cents with 6 coins.

2 Quarters, 1 dime, 2 nickels, and 1 penny. Answers may vary.

GEOGRAPHY

What is it called when a product is made in one country and sent to another country: imported or exported?

Exported

SCIENCE

True or False: The reason the sun sets and rises is because the sun moves around the Earth.

False

 **DID YOU KNOW?**

Plants grow from seeds. Write a poem about a plant that grows from a very small seed.

ANSWER KEY

LANGUAGE (correct this sentence)

mrs johnsons birthday is today she is very young

Mrs. Johnson's birthday is today. She is very young.

MATH

How many days are in the month of January?

31

GEOGRAPHY

What state does OK stand for?

Oklahoma

SCIENCE

Can plants grow in both hot and cold places?

Yes

 **DID YOU KNOW?**

Sometimes advice helps. Write advice for someone who had a fight with his or her best friend. Try to help the friends make up.

Learning Resources, Inc.   Daily Core Curriculum

Lesson 89

Name: _____

LANGUAGE (correct this sentence)
horrible harry is a character who is in 2th grade _____

MATH
Write a fact family for 2, 4, and 6.

SCIENCE
What is metamorphosis?

GEOGRAPHY
If I travel from North Carolina to Tennessee, which direction am I traveling?

DID YOU KNOW?
Snow falls from the sky. Write a poem about snow.

Lesson 90

Name: _____

LANGUAGE (correct this sentence)
the surprise will be at 830 pm, so please come to the party at 800

MATH
How many centimeters are in one decimeter?

SCIENCE
True or False: Magnets do not work in water.

GEOGRAPHY
Where is the Liberty Bell?

DID YOU KNOW?
Mosquitoes are harmful animals. Write a letter to a mosquito explaining why it would not want to bite you.

ANSWER KEY

Lesson 89

LANGUAGE (correct this sentence)

Horrible harry is a character who is in 2th grade

"Horrible Harry" is a character who is in 2nd grade.

MATH

Write a fact family for 2, 4, and 6.

2 + 4 = 6, 4 + 2 = 6, 6 - 2 = 4, 6 - 4 = 2

SCIENCE

What is metamorphosis?

Metamorphosis is the change that insects go through (e.g., a caterpillar changes into a butterfly).

GEOGRAPHY

If I travel from North Carolina to Tennessee, which direction am I traveling?

West

DID YOU KNOW?

Snow falls from the sky. Write a poem about snow.

ANSWER KEY

Lesson 90

LANGUAGE (correct this sentence)

The surprise will be at 830 pm, so please come to the party at 800

The surprise will be at 8:30 p.m., so please come to the party at 8:00.

MATH

How many centimeters are in one decimeter?

10 centimeters

SCIENCE

True or False: Magnets do not work in water.

False

GEOGRAPHY

Where is the Liberty Bell?

Philadelphia

DID YOU KNOW?

Mosquitoes are harmful animals. Write a letter to a mosquito explaining why it would not want to bite you.

© Learning Resources, Inc.

Daily Core Curriculum

Lesson 91

Name: _____

LANGUAGE (correct this address)
mrs scott dairy
100 cow lane
chocolate town RI 65987

_____
_____
_____

MATH
Finish the pattern:
4, 14, 24, ___, ___, ___, ___, ___

SCIENCE
Do caterpillars eat a lot before they turn into butterflies?

GEOGRAPHY
What country has these places: Peace River, Winnipeg, and Toronto?

DID YOU KNOW?
An island is a piece of land that is completely surrounded by water. List five things you might find on the islands of Hawaii.

Lesson 92

Name: _____

LANGUAGE (correct this sentence)
she is gonna get in trouble and then she will be sorry

MATH
June worked on her science project for 30 minutes on Wednesday. Then, she worked for an hour and a half on Thursday. How many hours did June work on her project?

SCIENCE
What has protons, neutrons, and electrons?

GEOGRAPHY
Is Bolivia a country or continent?

DID YOU KNOW?
Your teeth help you chomp up your food into little bits. Write a letter to the tooth fairy telling her when you think you will lose your next tooth.

ANSWER KEY

Lesson 91

LANGUAGE (correct this address)

~~mrs scott dairy~~
~~100 cow lane~~
~~chocolate town RI 65987~~

Mrs. Scott Dairy
100 Cow Lane
Chocolate Town, RI 65987

MATH
Finish the pattern:
14, 24, ___, ___, ___, ___, ___

34, 44, 54, 64, 74

GEOGRAPHY
What country has these places: Peace River, Winnipeg, and Toronto?

Canada

SCIENCE
Do caterpillars eat a lot before they turn into butterflies?

Yes

DID YOU KNOW?
An island is a piece of land that is completely surrounded by water. List five things you might find on the islands of Hawaii.

ANSWER KEY

Lesson 92

LANGUAGE (correct this sentence)

She is gonna get in trouble and then she will be sorry

She is going to get in trouble, and then she will be sorry.

MATH
June worked on her science project for 30 minutes on Wednesday. Then, she worked for an hour and a half on Thursday. How many hours did June work on her project?

2 hours

GEOGRAPHY
Is Bolivia a country or continent?

A country

SCIENCE
What has protons, neutrons, and electrons?

An atom

DID YOU KNOW?
Your teeth help you chomp up your food into little bits. Write a letter to the tooth fairy telling her when you think you will lose your next tooth.

© Learning Resources, Inc.   Daily Core Curriculum 95

Lesson 93

Name: _____

LANGUAGE (correct this sentence)
i am making a list of people to invite i will be sure to write bill carol ken dan and tom
_____

MATH
What shape is the bottom of a cylinder?

_____

SCIENCE
If I am able to recycle glass in my community, can I put my bottles in the recycling bin?

_____

GEOGRAPHY
Which state is known for its peaches?

_____

DID YOU KNOW?
Tuna, goldfish, and salmon are all kinds fish. Can you list three more? Describe what you think they look like.

Lesson 94

Name: _____

LANGUAGE (correct this sentence)
i laught when winnie the pooh got stuck in the window _____

MATH
What are the even numbers between 46 and 56?

_____

SCIENCE
Static electricity is caused by two charges positive and _____.

_____

GEOGRAPHY
What state has Concord as the capital city?

_____

DID YOU KNOW?
Rubber and cork will float in water. List five things that you think will float in water. Then, try it!

ANSWER KEY

LANGUAGE (correct this sentence)
i am making a list of people to invite i will be sure to write bill carol ken dan and tom
I am making a list of people to invite. I will be sure to write Bill, Carol, Ken, Dan, and Tom.

MATH
What shape is the bottom of a cylinder?

A circle

SCIENCE
If I am able to recycle glass in my community, can I put my bottles in the recycling bin?

Yes

GEOGRAPHY
Which state is known for its peaches?

Georgia

DID YOU KNOW?
Tuna, goldfish, and salmon are all kinds of fish. Can you list three more? Describe what you think they look like.

ANSWER KEY

LANGUAGE (correct this sentence)
i laught when winnie the pooh got stuck in the window
I laughed when Winnie the Pooh got stuck in the window.

MATH
What are the even numbers between 46 and 56?

48, 50, 52, 54

SCIENCE
Static electricity is caused by two charges: positive and _____.

Negative

GEOGRAPHY
What state has Concord as the capital city?

New Hampshire

DID YOU KNOW?
Rubber and cork will float in water. List five things that you think will float in water. Then, try it!

Lesson 95

Name: _____

LANGUAGE (correct this sentence)
dr hanson said to always brush my teeth before going to bed
_____

MATH
True or False: A square has four equal sides.

_____

SCIENCE
The three parts of the water cycle are: condensation, evaporation, and _____.

GEOGRAPHY
What is the abbreviation for Illinois?

_____

DID YOU KNOW?
Most insects are smaller than the tip of an adult pinky finger. Write about a time when you would like to be a fly on the wall.

Lesson 96

Name: _____

LANGUAGE (correct this sentence)
are you using youre best handwriting _____

MATH
The clay in the store comes in two sizes. Green clay weighs 2 pounds (.9 kg). Blue clay weighs 1 pound (.5 kg). Ted buys 1 package of green clay and 4 packages of blue clay. How many pounds of clay did Ted buy?

_____

SCIENCE
Should you eat more fat or more fruit daily

_____

GEOGRAPHY
What do you call more than one mountain together?

_____

DID YOU KNOW?
Practice makes perfect. What is something that you practice almost every day so you are better at it? Can you tell you have improved? Explain.

98 Daily Core Curriculum © Learning Resources,

ANSWER KEY

Lesson 95

LANGUAGE (correct this sentence)

dr hanson said to always brush my teeth before going to bed

Dr. Hanson said I should always brush my teeth before going to bed.

MATH

True or False: A square has four equal sides.

True

SCIENCE

The three parts of the water cycle are: condensation, evaporation, and _____.

Precipitation

GEOGRAPHY

What is the abbreviation for Illinois?

IL

DID YOU KNOW?

Most insects are smaller than the tip of an adult pinky finger. Write about a time when you would like to be a fly on the wall.

ANSWER KEY

Lesson 96

LANGUAGE (correct this sentence)

Are you using youre best handwriting

Are you using your best handwriting?

MATH

The clay in the store comes in two sizes. Green clay weighs 2 pounds (.9 kg). Blue clay weighs 1 pound (.5 kg). Ted buys 1 package of green clay and 4 packages of blue clay. How many pounds of clay did Ted buy?

6 pounds (2.7 kg)

SCIENCE

Should you eat more fat or more fruit daily?

Fruit

GEOGRAPHY

What do you call more than one mountain together?

A mountain range

DID YOU KNOW?

Practice makes perfect. What is something that you practice almost every day so you are better at it? Can you tell you have improved? Explain.

Lesson 97

Name: _____

LANGUAGE (correct this sentence)

please join i and wayne for dinner on tues _____

MATH
What month comes after January?

SCIENCE
If a sound is caused by a vibration, and the vibration stops, does the sound stop?

GEOGRAPHY
What ocean is to the east of the United States of America?

DID YOU KNOW?

Eskimos are called Inuits. Describe your perfect igloo. What would be inside?

Lesson 98

Name: _____

LANGUAGE (correct this sentence)

does you like chocolate and vanilla better _____

MATH
There were 2 pieces of pizza. Josh ate 1 of them. What fraction of the pizza did Josh eat?

SCIENCE
What kind of rocks are caused by change from pressure, heat, liquid, or gas?

GEOGRAPHY
What state has the abbreviation FL?

DID YOU KNOW?

A pond is bigger than a puddle. Write a story about a boy who finds a puddle. What does he do next?

ANSWER KEY

LANGUAGE (correct this sentence)

please join i and wayne for dinner on tues — **Please join Wayne and me for dinner on Tuesday.**

MATH

What month comes after January?

February

SCIENCE

If a sound is caused by a vibration, and the vibration stops, does the sound stop?

Yes

GEOGRAPHY

What ocean is to the east of the United States of America?

Atlantic Ocean

 **DID YOU KNOW?**

Eskimos are called Inuits. Describe your perfect igloo. What would be inside?

ANSWER KEY

LANGUAGE (correct this sentence)

does you like chocolate and vanilla better — **Do you like chocolate or vanilla better?**

MATH

There were 2 pieces of pizza. Josh ate 1 of them. What fraction of the pizza did Josh eat?

1/2

SCIENCE

What kind of rocks are caused by changes from pressure, heat, liquid, or gas?

Metamorphic rocks

GEOGRAPHY

What state has the abbreviation FL?

Florida

 **DID YOU KNOW?**

A pond is bigger than a puddle. Write a story about a boy who finds a puddle. What does he do next?

Learning Resources, Inc. Daily Core Curriculum

Lesson 99

Name: _____

LANGUAGE (correct this sentence)

id love to go to australia some day _____

MATH
Write the numbers from smallest to largest:
78, 968, 608, 28.

_____

SCIENCE
Which types of animals do NOT live in water: fish, frogs, or cats?

_____

GEOGRAPHY
Is Europe a country or continent?

_____

DID YOU KNOW?
Reptiles are cold-blooded. They like warm weather because their body temperature matches the weather! Would you want to live in the desert? Explain why or why not.

Lesson 100

Name: _____

LANGUAGE (correct this sentence)

lewis carroll was born on jan 27 1832 he wrote the book alice in wonderland

_____

MATH
What number is the Roman numeral IV?

_____

SCIENCE
What do deciduous trees do in the fall?

_____

GEOGRAPHY
Which state is nicknamed "The Bluegrass State"?

DID YOU KNOW?
Your five senses are seeing, hearing, smelling, tasting, and touching. Write about how you would use all of your senses on a hike.

ANSWER KEY

Lesson 99

LANGUAGE (correct this sentence)
I'd love to go to australia some day   **I'd love to go to Australia someday!**

MATH
Write the numbers from smallest to largest: 78, 968, 608, 28.

28, 78, 608, 968

SCIENCE
Which types of animals do NOT live in water: fish, frogs, or cats?

Cats

GEOGRAPHY
Is Europe a country or continent?

A continent

DID YOU KNOW?
Reptiles are cold-blooded. They like warm weather because their body temperature matches the weather! Would you want to live in the desert? Explain why or why not.

ANSWER KEY

Lesson 100

LANGUAGE (correct this sentence)
lewis Carroll was born on January 27, 1832. He wrote the book Alice in Wonderland.
Lewis Carroll was born on January 27, 1832. He wrote the book <u>Alice in Wonderland</u>.

MATH
What number is the Roman numeral IV?

4

SCIENCE
What do deciduous trees do in the fall?

They lose their leaves.

GEOGRAPHY
Which state is nicknamed "The Bluegrass State"?

Kentucky

DID YOU KNOW?
Your five senses are seeing, hearing, smelling, tasting, and touching. Write about how you would use all of your senses on a hike.

Daily Core Curriculum

Lesson 101

Name: _____

LANGUAGE (correct this sentence)
bill peet writed a lot of good books _____

MATH
Count by 6s from 0 to 24.

SCIENCE
Where does rain come from?

GEOGRAPHY
What states are on the West Coast of America?

DID YOU KNOW?
A smile makes everyone feel good. Imagine you smiled the whole day. Write how you might feel that day.

Lesson 102

Name: _____

LANGUAGE (correct this sentence)
do you write with your right hand or do you write with youre left hand

MATH
Danny bought Debbie 12 roses. Five of them were red. How many roses were not red?

SCIENCE
True or False: You can be struck by lightning on a rainy day.

GEOGRAPHY
True or False: Alaska touches the United States.

DID YOU KNOW?
Earth from space looks like a big globe with land, water, and clouds. Imagine you are traveling into space. What would you see?

ANSWER KEY

Lesson 101

LANGUAGE (correct this sentence)
ill peet writed a lot of good books   **Bill Peet wrote a lot of good books.**

MATH
Count by 6s from 0 to 24.

0, 6, 12, 18, 24

SCIENCE
Where does rain come from?

Rain comes from moisture in the clouds.

GEOGRAPHY
What states are on the West Coast of America?

California, Oregon, Washington

DID YOU KNOW?
A smile makes everyone feel good. Imagine you smiled the whole day. Write how you might feel that day.

ANSWER KEY

Lesson 102

LANGUAGE (correct this sentence)
do you write with your right hand or do you write with youre left hand
Do you write with your right hand or your left hand?

MATH
Danny bought Debbie 12 roses. Five of them were red. How many roses were not red?

7 roses

SCIENCE
True or False: You can be struck by lightning on a rainy day.

True

GEOGRAPHY
True or False: Alaska touches the United States.

False

DID YOU KNOW?
Earth from space looks like a big globe with land, water, and clouds. Imagine you are traveling into space. What would you see?

© Learning Resources, Inc.

Lesson 103

Name: _____

LANGUAGE (correct this sentence)

today is the fist day of february _____

MATH
What number comes after: 48?

SCIENCE
On what kind of plant do grapes grow?

GEOGRAPHY
Is Costa Rica a country or continent?

DID YOU KNOW?
The sun is a hot ball of gas. Write a story about someone who travels to the sun. Tell what he or she would have to wear and what might be on the sun.

Lesson 104

Name: _____

LANGUAGE (correct this sentence)

phil the groundhog likes to see his shadow _____

MATH
In the last 40 years, the groundhog saw his shadow 34 times. How many times did the groundhog NOT see his shadow? Write out the equation.

SCIENCE
Of the three zones of the ocean (sunlight, twilight, and deep-sea), which is the closest to the surface?

GEOGRAPHY
What state is known as "The Grand Canyon State"?

DID YOU KNOW?
Most insects have wings. Imagine you are flying on the back of a bee. What would you see and visit?

ANSWER KEY

Lesson 103

LANGUAGE (correct this sentence)

Today is the fist day of february   Today is the first day of February.

MATH
What number comes after: 48?

49

SCIENCE
On what kind of plant do grapes grow?

A vine

GEOGRAPHY
Is Costa Rica a country or continent?

A country

DID YOU KNOW?
The sun is a hot ball of gas. Write a story about someone who travels to the sun. Tell what he or she would have to wear and what might be on the sun.

ANSWER KEY

Lesson 104

LANGUAGE (correct this sentence)

phil the groundhog likes to see his shadow   Phil the groundhog likes to see his shadow.

MATH
In the last 40 years, the groundhog saw his shadow 34 times. How many times did the groundhog NOT see his shadow? Write out the equation.

40 − 34 = 6

SCIENCE
Of the three zones of the ocean (sunlight, twilight, and deep-sea), which is the closest to the surface?

Sunlight

GEOGRAPHY
What state is known as "The Grand Canyon State"?

Arizona

DID YOU KNOW?
Most insects have wings. Imagine you are flying on the back of a bee. What would you see and visit?

Daily Core Curriculum

Lesson 105

Name: _____

LANGUAGE (correct this sentence)

me and josh got cs on our test _____

MATH
Write a fact family for the following numbers: 8, 7, 15.

SCIENCE
If I am using the sense of smell, what part of my body am I using?

GEOGRAPHY
If I travel from Spain to Portugal, which direction will I travel?

DID YOU KNOW?
Native Americans taught the settlers how to grow corn. Write a letter to a friend describing step-by-step how to make your favorite snack.

Lesson 106

Name: _____

LANGUAGE (correct this sentence)

i was very loud when i sang the song happy birthday

MATH
What is the pattern: 15, 20, 25, 30, 35?

SCIENCE
Which climate is better for planting seeds in a garden: hot and sunny or cold and snowy?

GEOGRAPHY
What do we call a mountain that has poured out hot lava?

DID YOU KNOW?
A whale is a mammal. Imagine you are swimming around with a whale. What would it tell you to watch out for?

ANSWER KEY

Lesson 105

LANGUAGE (correct this sentence)
me and josh got cs on our test   **Josh and I got Cs on our test.**

MATH
Write a fact family for the following numbers: 8, 7, 15.

8 + 7 = 15 Answers will vary.

SCIENCE
If I am using the sense of smell, what part of my body am I using?

Nose

GEOGRAPHY
If I travel from Spain to Portugal, which direction will I travel?

West

DID YOU KNOW?
Native Americans taught the settlers how to grow corn. Write a letter to a friend describing step-by-step how to make your favorite snack.

ANSWER KEY

Lesson 106

LANGUAGE (correct this sentence)
I was very loud when i sang the song happy birthday
I was very loud when I sang the song "Happy Birthday."

MATH
What is the pattern: 15, 20, 25, 30, 35?

5 more

SCIENCE
Which climate is better for planting seeds in a garden: hot and sunny or cold and snowy?

Hot and sunny

GEOGRAPHY
What do we call a mountain that has poured out hot lava?

Volcano

DID YOU KNOW?
A whale is a mammal. Imagine you are swimming around with a whale. What would it tell you to watch out for?

Lesson 107

Name: _____

LANGUAGE (correct this sentence)
come join gina and i at 200 pm _____

MATH
How many weeks are in one year?

SCIENCE
What is at the center of our solar system?

GEOGRAPHY
What state has the abbreviation NC?

DID YOU KNOW?
Christopher Columbus was from Spain. Write a diary entry from Christopher Columbus on what he would see if he visited America today.

Lesson 108

Name: _____

LANGUAGE (correct this sentence)
on mondays we go to art class _____

MATH
How many ways can you make 30 cents using pennies, nickels, dimes, and quarters? Write down as many ways as you can.

SCIENCE
True or False: Spiders are insects.

GEOGRAPHY
How many continents are there?

DID YOU KNOW?
President Ronald Reagan was born in 191 in Illinois. What do you think you would find in Illinois? Write about it.

ANSWER KEY

Lesson 107

LANGUAGE (correct this sentence)
come join gina and i at 200 pm   Come join Gina and me at 2:00 p.m.

MATH
How many weeks are in one year?

52 weeks

GEOGRAPHY
What state has the abbreviation NC?

North Carolina

SCIENCE
What is at the center of our solar system?

The sun

DID YOU KNOW?
Christopher Columbus was from Spain. Write a diary entry from Christopher Columbus on what he would see if he visited America today.

ANSWER KEY

Lesson 108

LANGUAGE (correct this sentence)
on mondays we go to art class   On Mondays we go to art class.

MATH
How many ways can you make 30 cents using pennies, nickels, dimes, and quarters? Write down as many ways as you can.

Answers will vary.

GEOGRAPHY
How many continents are there?

7 continents

SCIENCE
True or False: Spiders are insects.

False

DID YOU KNOW?
President Ronald Reagan was born in 1911 in Illinois. What do you think you would find in Illinois? Write about it.

Learning Resources, Inc.   Daily Core Curriculum

Lesson 109

Name: _____

LANGUAGE (correct this sentence)
aunt belinda larsen
1234 lovely way
clearwater fl 65498

MATH
Today is February 7. How many days are left in February?

SCIENCE
Is the heart an organ?

GEOGRAPHY
True or False: Lakes were created by glaciers.

DID YOU KNOW?

Learning a new language is hard work! Imagine you are learning English for the first time. What do you think would be the hardest for someone who does not speak it

---

Lesson 110

Name: _____

LANGUAGE (correct this sentence)
please buy milk eggs and corn at the grocery store

MATH
Count back by ones:
66, 65, ___, ___, ___, ___, ___, ___, ___

SCIENCE
List ways you used your sense of taste this morning.

GEOGRAPHY
In which state is Hartford the capital city?

DID YOU KNOW?

Yeast in dough rises. Write a recipe for being a kid. Include measurements like 1/4 cup fun, 1/3 cup friends, etc.

ANSWER KEY

Lesson 109

LANGUAGE (correct this sentence)

aunt belinda larsen
1234 lovely way
clearwater fl 65498

Aunt Belinda Larsen
1234 Lovely Way
Clearwater, FL 65498

MATH

Today is February 7. How many days are left in February?

21 usually, 22 with a leap year

SCIENCE

Is the heart an organ?

Yes

GEOGRAPHY

True or False: Lakes were created by glaciers.

True

DID YOU KNOW?

Learning a new language is hard work! Imagine you are learning English for the first time. What do you think would be the hardest for someone who does not speak it?

ANSWER KEY

Lesson 110

LANGUAGE (correct this sentence)

please buy milk eggs and corn at the grocery store

Please buy milk, eggs, and corn at the grocery store.

MATH

Count back by ones:
66, 65, ___, ___, ___, ___, ___, ___, ___

64, 63, 62, 61, 60, 59, 58

SCIENCE

List ways you used your sense of taste this morning.

Answers will vary.

GEOGRAPHY

In which state is Hartford the capital city?

Connecticut

DID YOU KNOW?

Yeast in dough rises. Write a recipe for being a kid. Include measurements like 1/4 cup fun, 1/3 cup friends, etc.

Learning Resources, Inc. Daily Core Curriculum 113

Lesson 111

Name: _____

LANGUAGE (correct this sentence)
i wish my dog could talk she would say funny things _____

MATH
What is a hexagon?

SCIENCE
True or False: An insect's skeleton is on the outside of its body.

GEOGRAPHY
Where is the Taj Mahal?

DID YOU KNOW?
Thomas Edison invented the light bulb. Write about something you would like to invent.

Lesson 112

Name: _____

LANGUAGE (correct this sentence)
what happened to your sisters slipper _____

MATH
When I'm measuring liquids, would I use meter or liter?

SCIENCE
Are dinosaurs extinct?

GEOGRAPHY
Which state has the Empire State building?

DID YOU KNOW?
Abraham Lincoln's nickname was Honest Abe. Write about one of your nicknames and how you got it.

ANSWER KEY

Lesson 111

LANGUAGE (correct this sentence)
i wish my dog could talk she would say funny things

I wish my dog could talk. She would say funny things.

MATH
What is a hexagon?

A six-sided figure

SCIENCE
True or False: An insect's skeleton is on the outside of its body.

True

GEOGRAPHY
Where is the Taj Mahal?

In India

 **DID YOU KNOW?**
Thomas Edison invented the light bulb. Write about something you would like to invent.

ANSWER KEY

Lesson 112

LANGUAGE (correct this sentence)
what happened to your sisters slipper

What happened to your sister's slipper?

MATH
When I'm measuring liquids, would I use meter or liter?

Liter

SCIENCE
Are dinosaurs extinct?

Yes

GEOGRAPHY
Which state has the Empire State building?

New York

 **DID YOU KNOW?**
Abraham Lincoln's nickname was Honest Abe. Write about one of your nicknames and how you got it.

Learning Resources, Inc. Daily Core Curriculum 115

Lesson 113

Name: _____

LANGUAGE (correct this sentence)

my mother said go wash up before dinner _____

MATH

What number has 7 hundreds, 9 tens, and 5 ones?

_____

SCIENCE

Are birds and mammals related?

_____

GEOGRAPHY

Is Delaware a city or state?

_____

DID YOU KNOW?

Water evaporates as a gas into the air and turns into water again in clouds. Write about the last big storm you were in. What were you doing, and how did you take shelter?

✂···

Lesson 114

Name: _____

LANGUAGE (correct this sentence)

valentines day is a fun day for friends _____

MATH

Charese was signing her Valentine cards. She had already signed 20. There were 16 more to go. How many did she have altogether?

_____

SCIENCE

True or False: Plants use the air we breathe out.

_____

GEOGRAPHY

What is a skyscraper?

_____

DID YOU KNOW?

A bone that breaks needs to be set in a cast. Did you ever break a bone or did a friend or family member? Describe what happened.

ANSWER KEY

 Lesson 113

LANGUAGE (correct this sentence)

my mother said go wash up before dinner   **My mother said, "Go wash up before dinner."**

MATH

What number has 7 hundreds, 9 tens, and 5 ones?

795

GEOGRAPHY

Is Delaware a city or state?

A state

SCIENCE

Are birds and mammals related?

No

DID YOU KNOW?

Water evaporates as a gas into the air and turns into water again in clouds. Write about the last big storm you were in. What were you doing, and how did you take shelter?

ANSWER KEY

 Lesson 114

LANGUAGE (correct this sentence)

valentines day is a fun day for friends   **Valentine's Day is a fun day for friends.**

MATH

Charese was signing her Valentine cards. She had already signed 20. There were 16 more to go. How many did she have together?

36

SCIENCE

True or False: Plants use the air we breathe out.

True

GEOGRAPHY

What is a skyscraper?

A very tall building

DID YOU KNOW?

A bone that breaks needs to be set in a cast. Did you ever break a bone or did a friend or family member? Describe what happened.

Learning Resources, Inc.   Daily Core Curriculum

Lesson 115

Name: _____

LANGUAGE (correct this sentence)
today is friday february 15 2003 _____

MATH
42 + 63 =

SCIENCE
True or False: Snakes and toads are both reptiles.

GEOGRAPHY
Name two continents.

DID YOU KNOW?
"Butterflies in your stomach" means that you are nervous. When was the last time you had butterflies in your stomach? Explain why.

Lesson 116

Name: _____

LANGUAGE (correct this sentence)
we will go to class at 900 am _____

MATH
Write these numbers from largest to smallest: 564, 586, 508, 5,000.

SCIENCE
Is Pluto a planet?

GEOGRAPHY
Name the ocean near the East Coast of America.

DID YOU KNOW?
People who move from far away are called immigrants in their new land. Would you want to live in another country? Explain which country you would choose.

ANSWER KEY

Lesson 115

LANGUAGE (correct this sentence)
Today is friday february 15 2003 — **Today is Friday, February 15, 2003.**

MATH
2 + 63=

105

GEOGRAPHY
Name two continents.

Answers will vary.

SCIENCE
True or False: Snakes and toads are both reptiles.

False

DID YOU KNOW?
"Butterflies in your stomach" means that you are nervous. When was the last time you had butterflies in your stomach? Explain why.

ANSWER KEY

Lesson 116

LANGUAGE (correct this sentence)
We will go to class at 900 am — **We will go to class at 9:00 a.m.**

MATH
Write these numbers from largest to smallest: 564, 586, 508, 5,000.

5,000, 586, 564, 508

GEOGRAPHY
Name the ocean near the East Coast of America.

Atlantic Ocean

SCIENCE
Is Pluto a planet?

Yes

DID YOU KNOW?
People who move from far away are called immigrants in their new land. Would you want to live in another country? Explain which country you would choose.

Learning Resources, Inc. Daily Core Curriculum

Lesson 117

Name: _____

LANGUAGE (correct this sentence)
what is yer name _____

MATH
You made one 2-point basket and one 3-point basket. How many points did you score for your team?

SCIENCE
If I plant a sunflower seed, what will grow?

GEOGRAPHY
Which state has Lake Okeechobee?

DID YOU KNOW?
It takes 365 days for Earth to go around the sun once. Invent a machine so the Earth can go around the sun faster. Describe what it would include.

Lesson 118

Name: _____

LANGUAGE (correct this sentence)
i could have gone with my dad to work _____

MATH
Write all of the even numbers between 100 and 113.

SCIENCE
True or False: Precipitation is rain, sleet, snow, and ice.

GEOGRAPHY
What continent does Argentina belong to?

DID YOU KNOW?
Birds often build their homes in trees and other high places. Imagine you could have a tree house. What would be inside? Would you have a secret code to get in?

120 Daily Core Curriculum © Learning Resources,

ANSWER KEY

Lesson 117

LANGUAGE (correct this sentence)

whats yer name   **What is your name?**

MATH

You made one 2-point basket and one 3-point basket. How many points did you score for your team?

5 points

SCIENCE

If I plant a sunflower seed, what will grow?

Sunflowers

GEOGRAPHY

Which state has Lake Okeechobee?

Florida

DID YOU KNOW?

It takes 365 days for Earth to go around the sun once. Invent a machine so the Earth can go around the sun faster. Describe what it would include.

ANSWER KEY

Lesson 118

LANGUAGE (correct this sentence)

i could have gone with my dad to work   **I could have gone with my dad to work.**

MATH

Write all of the even numbers between 100 and 113.

102, 104, 106, 108, 110, 112

SCIENCE

True or False: Precipitation is rain, sleet, snow, and ice.

True

GEOGRAPHY

What continent does Argentina belong to?

South America

DID YOU KNOW?

Birds often build their homes in trees and other high places. Imagine you could have a tree house. What would be inside? Would you have a secret code to get in?

★ Lesson 119

Name: _____

LANGUAGE (correct this sentence)
who bringed there jacket on the bus _____

MATH
Count back by 10s: 98, 88, ___, ___, ___, ___, ___, ___, ___

SCIENCE
Is a Brachiosaurus an herbivore (eats plants), a carnivore (eats meat), or an omnivore (eats both plants and meat)?

GEOGRAPHY
What is the constitution of the United States?

DID YOU KNOW?

Prey is an animal that is hunted by a predator for food. Write a letter to a mouse, telling it why it should not go into the forest at night.

★ Lesson 120

Name: _____

LANGUAGE (correct this sentence)
we will get an ice cream cone later _____

MATH
Roxanne is using milk to go with her cereal. About how much milk will she use: 1 cup, 1 gallon, or 1 kilogram?

SCIENCE
True or False: A wheel lets a car move.

GEOGRAPHY
What type of body of water is partly enclosed by land?

DID YOU KNOW?

Your skeletal system keeps you upright, just like the poles in a tent. Imagine if you did not have bones. Write what life would be like.

ANSWER KEY

Lesson 119

LANGUAGE (correct this sentence)
who bringed there jacket on the bus   Who brought their jacket on the bus?

MATH
count back by 10s: 98, 88, ___, ___, ___, ___, ___, ___, ___

78, 68, 58, 48, 38, 28, 18

SCIENCE
Is a Brachiosaurus an herbivore (eats plants), a carnivore (eats meat), or an omnivore (eats both plants and meat)?

An herbivore

GEOGRAPHY
What is the constitution of the United States?

A list of laws to live by

DID YOU KNOW?
Prey is an animal that is hunted by a predator for food. Write a letter to a mouse, telling it why it should not go into the forest at night.

ANSWER KEY

Lesson 120

LANGUAGE (correct this sentence)
well get a ice cream cone later   We will get an ice cream cone later.

MATH
Roxanne is using milk to go with her cereal. About how much milk will she use: 1 cup, 1 gallon, or 1 kilogram?

1 cup

SCIENCE
True or False: A wheel lets a car move.

True

GEOGRAPHY
What type of body of water is partly enclosed by land?

A bay or gulf

DID YOU KNOW?
Your skeletal system keeps you upright, just like the poles in a tent. Imagine if you did not have bones. Write what life would be like.

Learning Resources, Inc.   Daily Core Curriculum

LESSON 1 QUIZ (Lessons 1-10)

Shade in the correct answer.

LANGUAGE ARTS

1. I am in second grade
   - Ⓐ I am in second grade,
   - Ⓑ I am in second grade?
   - Ⓒ I am in second grade.
   - Ⓓ Correct as is

2. there are thirty days in september
   - Ⓐ There are Thirty days in september.
   - Ⓑ There are thirty days in September.
   - Ⓒ There is thirty days in September.
   - Ⓓ Correct as is

3. shes sitting down
   - Ⓐ She is sitting down
   - Ⓑ She is sitting down!
   - Ⓒ She is sitting down,
   - Ⓓ She is sitting down.

MATH

4. How much money is one dime?
   - Ⓐ 5 cents
   - Ⓑ 10 cents
   - Ⓒ 25 cents
   - Ⓓ 50 cents

5. There were 9 apples. 7 of them had worms. How many apples were without worms?
   - Ⓐ 2 apples
   - Ⓑ 7 apples
   - Ⓒ 9 apples
   - Ⓓ 4 apples

6. 5 children were playing. 3 left. How many children were still playing?
   - Ⓐ 5 children
   - Ⓑ 3 children
   - Ⓒ 2 children
   - Ⓓ 1 child

SCIENCE

7. Which is not a tree?
   - Ⓐ Maple
   - Ⓑ Oak
   - Ⓒ Willow
   - Ⓓ Daisy

8. How is the temperature measured?
   - Ⓐ Compass
   - Ⓑ Thermometer
   - Ⓒ Balance
   - Ⓓ Ruler

9. What is something you cannot recycle?
   - Ⓐ Pop can
   - Ⓑ Plastic bottle
   - Ⓒ Newspaper
   - Ⓓ Food

GEOGRAPHY

10. What is the capital of the United States of America?
    - Ⓐ Springfield
    - Ⓑ Washington, D.C.
    - Ⓒ Arlington
    - Ⓓ St. Louis

11. Rivers, lakes, and oceans are all bodies of water.
    - Ⓐ True
    - Ⓑ False

12. There are two poles on the Earth.
    - Ⓐ True
    - Ⓑ False

LESSON 2 QUIZ (Lessons 11–20)

...ade in the correct answer.

LANGUAGE ARTS

...two people is going tonight
- Ⓐ Two people is going tonight.
- Ⓑ Two people are going tonight.
- Ⓒ Two people are going tonight
- Ⓓ Correct as is

...where is mine book it was on the table yesterday
- Ⓐ Where is mine book. It was on the table yesterday.
- Ⓑ Where is my book? It was on the table yesterday.
- Ⓒ Where my book? It was on the table Yesterday.
- Ⓓ Correct as is

...what did Jennifer say about the game
- Ⓐ What did Jennifer say about the game.
- Ⓑ What did Jennifer say about the Game.
- Ⓒ What did Jennifer say about the game?
- Ⓓ Correct as is

MATH

...What number has 7 tens and 0 ones?
- Ⓐ 70
- Ⓑ 07
- Ⓒ 700
- Ⓓ 7,000

...What is 427 pennies in dollars and cents?
- Ⓐ $4.27
- Ⓑ $472
- Ⓒ $427
- Ⓓ $4.00

...How many sides are on an octagon?
- Ⓐ 5
- Ⓑ 6
- Ⓒ 8
- Ⓓ 10

SCIENCE

7. What kind of reptiles lived millions of years ago?
   - Ⓐ Snakes
   - Ⓑ Alligators
   - Ⓒ Dinosaurs
   - Ⓓ Crocodiles

8. What kind of animal is warm-blooded and takes care of its young?
   - Ⓐ Mammal
   - Ⓑ Reptile
   - Ⓒ Amphibian
   - Ⓓ None of the above

9. What kind of matter is water?
   - Ⓐ Liquid
   - Ⓑ Solid
   - Ⓒ Gas
   - Ⓓ Cloud

GEOGRAPHY

10. On which continent is Mexico?
    - Ⓐ North America
    - Ⓑ South America
    - Ⓒ Europe
    - Ⓓ Asia

11. How many equators are on Earth?
    - Ⓐ One
    - Ⓑ Two
    - Ⓒ Three
    - Ⓓ Zero

12. What continent and country have the same name?
    - Ⓐ Europe
    - Ⓑ Asia
    - Ⓒ North America
    - Ⓓ Australia

Learning Resources, Inc.   Daily Core Curriculum

LESSON 3 QUIZ (Lessons 21-30)

Shade in the correct answer.

LANGUAGE ARTS

1. marcia and jan bringed there bikes to school
   - Ⓐ Marcia and Jan bringed their bikes to school.
   - Ⓑ Marcia and jan brought there bikes to school.
   - Ⓒ Marcia and Jan, they brought their bikes to school.
   - Ⓓ Marcia and Jan brought their bikes to school.

2. she will go two there house at 1200 pm
   - Ⓐ She will go to their house at 12:00 p.m.
   - Ⓑ She went to go to their house at 12:00 p.m.
   - Ⓒ She has gone to their house at 12:00 pm
   - Ⓓ She goes to their house at 12:00 pm

3. i went to columbus ohio last august
   - Ⓐ I went to Columbus, Ohio last august
   - Ⓑ I went to columbus, ohio last august.
   - Ⓒ I went to Columbus, Ohio last August.
   - Ⓓ Correct as is

MATH

4. 3 sisters, 3 brothers, and 2 parents are how many people total in the family?
   - Ⓐ 7
   - Ⓑ 8
   - Ⓒ 9
   - Ⓓ 10

5. John has 22 baseball cards. He sells 10. How many are left?
   - Ⓐ 10
   - Ⓑ 12
   - Ⓒ 11
   - Ⓓ None of the above

6. Are the numbers 3, 7, 9, and 13 even or odd?
   - Ⓐ Even
   - Ⓑ Odd

SCIENCE

7. What do you call moving air?
   - Ⓐ Wind
   - Ⓑ Wave
   - Ⓒ Rain
   - Ⓓ None of the above

8. What is it called when animals can blend in with their surroundings?
   - Ⓐ Feathers
   - Ⓑ Lost
   - Ⓒ Camouflage
   - Ⓓ Texture

9. What is the source of heat and light for Earth?
   - Ⓐ Moon
   - Ⓑ Pluto
   - Ⓒ Sun
   - Ⓓ Comets

GEOGRAPHY

10. On what continent is Italy located?
    - Ⓐ Asia
    - Ⓑ North America
    - Ⓒ Australia
    - Ⓓ Europe

11. IL is the abbreviation for which state?
    - Ⓐ Illinois
    - Ⓑ Indiana
    - Ⓒ Iowa
    - Ⓓ Louisiana

12. How is a map key used?
    - Ⓐ To label sites
    - Ⓑ For reading a map
    - Ⓒ For learning about an area
    - Ⓓ All of the above

LESSON 4 QUIZ (Lessons 31-40)

...ade in the correct answer.

LANGUAGE ARTS

i and susan is going to school today
- Ⓐ Susan and I are going to school today.
- Ⓑ Me and susan are going to school today
- Ⓒ Susan and me, we are going to school today.
- Ⓓ Correct as is

stop pushing me shouted gillian
- Ⓐ "Stop pushing me," shouted gillian.
- Ⓑ Stop pushing me shouted Gillian
- Ⓒ Stop pushing me, shouted Gillian!
- Ⓓ "Stop pushing me!" shouted Gillian.

henry says it is gonna rain this afternoon
- Ⓐ Henry says, "It is going to rain this afternoon."
- Ⓑ Henry says, It is going to rain this afternoon
- Ⓒ henry says, "is going to rain this afternoon."
- Ⓓ Henry says it is going to rain this afternoon

MATH

40 + 20 = ?
- Ⓐ 6
- Ⓑ 60
- Ⓒ 20
- Ⓓ 70

Which number is greater: 123 or 321?
- Ⓐ 123
- Ⓑ 321

What number is the Roman numeral X?
- Ⓐ 7
- Ⓑ 5
- Ⓒ 15
- Ⓓ 10

SCIENCE

7. What sense are you using if you use your eyes?
- Ⓐ Sense of touch
- Ⓑ Sense of taste
- Ⓒ Sense of sight
- Ⓓ Sense of smell

8. Alligators are reptiles and crocodiles are not.
- Ⓐ True
- Ⓑ False

9. Earth is the ___ planet away from the sun.
- Ⓐ Third
- Ⓑ Ninth
- Ⓒ Fifth
- Ⓓ Seventh

GEOGRAPHY

10. What do we call the largest bodies of water?
- Ⓐ Lakes
- Ⓑ Oceans
- Ⓒ Bays
- Ⓓ Rivers

11. What large lake can be found in Utah?
- Ⓐ Utah Lake
- Ⓑ Canyon Lake
- Ⓒ Salt Lake
- Ⓓ Lake Tahoe

12. Which one is human-made?
- Ⓐ An ocean
- Ⓑ A building
- Ⓒ A volcano
- Ⓓ A river

LESSON 5 QUIZ (Lessons 41–50)

Shade in the correct answer.

LANGUAGE ARTS

1. on jan 4, i will go to canada
   - Ⓐ On January 4, I will go to canada.
   - Ⓑ On January 4, I will go to Canada.
   - Ⓒ On January 4 i go to canada
   - Ⓓ Correct as is

2. jodi saw the spider and screamed yikes
   - Ⓐ Jodi saw the spider and screamed yikes.
   - Ⓑ Jodi saw the spider and screamed, "Yikes!"
   - Ⓒ Jodi saw the spider, and then she screamed.
   - Ⓓ Jodie saw the spider, and it screamed "yikes."

3. arthur is a character in marc browns books
   - Ⓐ Arthur is a character in marc brown's books
   - Ⓑ Arthur is a character in marc Brown's books.
   - Ⓒ Arthur, he is a character.
   - Ⓓ Arthur is a character in Marc Brown's books.

MATH

4. What number has 9 hundreds, 6 tens, and 2 ones?
   - Ⓐ 92
   - Ⓑ 96
   - Ⓒ 962
   - Ⓓ 296

5. Jennings collected 27 pieces of candy. Then, he got 38 more. How many pieces of candy did he collect in all?
   - Ⓐ 65
   - Ⓑ 60
   - Ⓒ 68
   - Ⓓ 70

6. How much is one nickel worth?
   - Ⓐ 1 cent
   - Ⓑ 5 cents
   - Ⓒ 10 cents
   - Ⓓ 25 cents

SCIENCE

7. How many suns are there in our solar system?
   - Ⓐ 3 suns
   - Ⓑ 1 sun
   - Ⓒ 2 suns
   - Ⓓ No suns

8. Cups can be used to measure solids (like powder) or liquids (like water).
   - Ⓐ True
   - Ⓑ False

9. What is a plant from which you can eat the leaves?
   - Ⓐ Lettuce
   - Ⓑ Fern
   - Ⓒ Tomato
   - Ⓓ Ivy

GEOGRAPHY

10. In what state is the Statue of Liberty?
    - Ⓐ New Hampshire
    - Ⓑ Delaware
    - Ⓒ New York
    - Ⓓ Maine

11. Which country is in South America?
    - Ⓐ Spain
    - Ⓑ Korea
    - Ⓒ Peru
    - Ⓓ Mexico

12. If you travel from Mexico to Canada, which direction will you be traveling?
    - Ⓐ North
    - Ⓑ South
    - Ⓒ East
    - Ⓓ West

LESSON 6 QUIZ (Lessons 51-60)

...ade in the correct answer.

LANGUAGE ARTS

juanita bringed the chips and dip to the party
- Ⓐ Juanita brought the chips and dip for the party"
- Ⓑ Juanita done bring the chips and dip to the party
- Ⓒ Juanita brought the chips and dip to the party.
- Ⓓ Correct as is

lynnae like going going two school
- Ⓐ Lynnae likes going too school
- Ⓑ Lynnae like to go to scool.
- Ⓒ Lynnae likes going to school.
- Ⓓ Correct as is

how fast can pauline write those letters
- Ⓐ how fast can pauline write those letters.
- Ⓑ How fast can Pauline write those letters?
- Ⓒ How fast can she write letters?
- Ⓓ How fast can Pauline write those letters.

MATH

There were 23 blue corn chips and 65 potato chips. How many chips altogether?
- Ⓐ 88 chips
- Ⓑ 42 chips
- Ⓒ 23 chips
- Ⓓ 80 chips

What is NOT a fact family for the numbers 3, 4, and 7?
- Ⓐ $7 - 3 = 4$
- Ⓑ $7 + 3 = 10$
- Ⓒ $3 + 4 = 7$
- Ⓓ $7 - 4 = 3$

What number is the Roman numeral II?
- Ⓐ 2
- Ⓑ 4
- Ⓒ 6
- Ⓓ 8

SCIENCE

7. What is something a plant does not need in order to grow?
- Ⓐ Water
- Ⓑ Sunlight
- Ⓒ Air
- Ⓓ Curtains

8. The needle on a compass always points north.
- Ⓐ True
- Ⓑ False

9. Which is not a type of rock?
- Ⓐ Igneous
- Ⓑ Sedimentary
- Ⓒ Metamorphic
- Ⓓ Larvae

GEOGRAPHY

10. What kind of body of water is the Atlantic?
- Ⓐ Buy
- Ⓑ Gulf
- Ⓒ River
- Ⓓ Ocean

11. What state is abbreviated MO?
- Ⓐ Missouri
- Ⓑ Ohio
- Ⓒ Maine
- Ⓓ New Mexico

12. What body of water is to the west of Florida?
- Ⓐ Atlantic Ocean
- Ⓑ Gulf of Mexico
- Ⓒ Lake Ontario
- Ⓓ Connecticut River

LESSON 7 QUIZ (Lessons 61-70)

Shade in the correct answer.

LANGUAGE ARTS

1. what is your favorite dessert
   - Ⓐ What is your favorite dessert?
   - Ⓑ What! Your favorite dessert?
   - Ⓒ What is your favorite dessert.
   - Ⓓ What is your favorite dessert!

2. december is my favorite month what is yours
   - Ⓐ December is my favorite Month. What is yours?
   - Ⓑ December is my favorite month. What is yours.
   - Ⓒ December is my favorite month? What is yours.
   - Ⓓ December is my favorite month. What is yours?

3. mom and dad went to the university of iowa
   - Ⓐ Mom and Dad went to the university of iowa.
   - Ⓑ Mom and dad went to the university of Iowa.
   - Ⓒ Mom and Dad went to the University of Iowa.
   - Ⓓ Correct as is

MATH

4. How can you make 40 cents?
   - Ⓐ 4 dimes
   - Ⓑ 5 nickels
   - Ⓒ 19 pennies
   - Ⓓ 1 quarter

5. Thomas weighs 53 pounds. Emily weighs 51 pounds. What is the sum of Thomas and Emily's weight?
   - Ⓐ 110 pounds
   - Ⓑ 2 pounds
   - Ⓒ 104 pounds
   - Ⓓ 94 pounds

6. Put any needed commas in this number: 76431.
   - Ⓐ 7,6431
   - Ⓑ 764,31
   - Ⓒ 76,4,31
   - Ⓓ 76,431

SCIENCE

7. Magnets attract all types of metal.
   - Ⓐ True
   - Ⓑ False

8. A duck swims to find its food. A woodpecker looks for insects on trees. Which of these birds needs webbed feet?
   - Ⓐ A duck needs webbed feet.
   - Ⓑ A woodpecker needs webbed feet.

9. Finish this sentence: A caterpillar will turn into a _____
   - Ⓐ Fly
   - Ⓑ Spider
   - Ⓒ Beetle
   - Ⓓ Butterfly

GEOGRAPHY

10. Which is bigger?
    - Ⓐ Cuba
    - Ⓑ Alaska

11. Name the continent: Canada, Rocky Mountains, Great Lakes.
    - Ⓐ Europe
    - Ⓑ Asia
    - Ⓒ Australia
    - Ⓓ North America

12. You can travel to Japan from the United States by car.
    - Ⓐ True
    - Ⓑ False

LESSON 8 QUIZ (Lessons 71-80)

ade in the correct answer.

LANGUAGE ARTS

who goes with the teacher at 300 pm, is it george or martha
- Ⓐ Who goes with the teacher at 3:00 p.m., is it George or martha?
- Ⓑ Who goes with the teacher at 3:00 p.m.? Is it George or Martha?
- Ⓒ Who goes with the teacher at 3:00 pm, is it George or Martha?
- Ⓓ Correct as is

the snowfall maked it very hard to drive
- Ⓐ the snowfall made it very hard to drive.
- Ⓑ the snowfall made it very hard to drive
- Ⓒ The snowfall made it very hard to drive"
- Ⓓ The snowfall made it very hard to drive.

What is the abbreviation for street?
- Ⓐ what is the abbreviation for street!
- Ⓑ What is the abbreviation for street.
- Ⓒ Where is the abbreviation for street?
- Ⓓ Correct as is

MATH

. The table length is 3 feet. How many yards is that?
- Ⓐ 2 yards
- Ⓑ 3 yards
- Ⓒ 1 yard
- Ⓓ 0 yards

. What shape is a stop sign?
- Ⓐ Diamond
- Ⓑ Pentagon
- Ⓒ Triangle
- Ⓓ Octagon

. Finish the pattern: 11, 22, 33, 44, ___, ___, ___
- Ⓐ 44, 64, 74
- Ⓑ 55, 66, 77
- Ⓒ 54, 55, 56
- Ⓓ 55, 60, 70

SCIENCE

7. Is paper towel recyclable?
- Ⓐ Yes
- Ⓑ No

8. Which is NOT used to find out the weather?
- Ⓐ Thermometer
- Ⓑ Barometer
- Ⓒ Kilometer
- Ⓓ Satellites

9. Finish this sentence: After lightning, you hear _____.
- Ⓐ Clouds
- Ⓑ Rainbows
- Ⓒ Thunder
- Ⓓ Horns

GEOGRAPHY

10. What is China?
- Ⓐ A continent
- Ⓑ A lake
- Ⓒ A country
- Ⓓ A state

11. Which are the largest?
- Ⓐ Ponds
- Ⓑ Lakes
- Ⓒ Rivers
- Ⓓ Oceans

12. What are continents?
- Ⓐ Large bodies of water
- Ⓑ Large bodies of land
- Ⓒ A very small hill
- Ⓓ Another name for the United States

LESSON 9 QUIZ (Lessons 81-90)

Shade in the correct answer.

LANGUAGE ARTS

1. zach and me is going out to lunch tomorrow
    - Ⓐ Zach and I are going out to lunch tomorrow.
    - Ⓑ Zach and we are going out to lunch tomorrow.
    - Ⓒ Me and Zach, we are going to lunch tomorrow.
    - Ⓓ Correct as is

2. what day of the week comes after thurs
    - Ⓐ What day of the Week comes after Thursday?
    - Ⓑ What day of the week comes after thursday.
    - Ⓒ What day of the week comes after Thursday?
    - Ⓓ What day of the week comes after thursday

3. the class votes for a new president tomorrow
    - Ⓐ The class votes for a new president tomorrow.
    - Ⓑ the Class votes for a new President tomorrow.
    - Ⓒ the class they vote for a new president tomorrow.
    - Ⓓ Correct as is

MATH

4. What number has 4 tens, 6 ones, and 8 hundreds?
    - Ⓐ 468
    - Ⓑ 4,680
    - Ⓒ 864
    - Ⓓ 846

5. Write the numbers from largest to smallest: 123, 564, 103, 524.
    - Ⓐ 524, 103, 123, 564
    - Ⓑ 564, 524, 123, 103
    - Ⓒ 103, 123, 564, 524
    - Ⓓ 103, 123, 523, 564

6. What is not a fact family for 2, 4, and 6?
    - Ⓐ 6 − 4 = 2
    - Ⓑ 6 − 2 = 4
    - Ⓒ 4 + 3 = 7
    - Ⓓ 4 + 2 = 6

SCIENCE

7. Can plants grow in wet and dry places?
    - Ⓐ Yes
    - Ⓑ No

8. What type of rock is formed when magma from inside the Earth cools and hardens?
    - Ⓐ Sedimentary
    - Ⓑ Igneous
    - Ⓒ Metamorphic
    - Ⓓ None of the above

9. The reason why the sun sets and rises is because the sun moves around the Earth.
    - Ⓐ True
    - Ⓑ False

GEOGRAPHY

10. Which is a city?
    - Ⓐ Colorado
    - Ⓑ Illinois
    - Ⓒ Boston
    - Ⓓ Tennessee

11. On what continent is India?
    - Ⓐ Europe
    - Ⓑ Australia
    - Ⓒ Africa
    - Ⓓ Asia

12. If you travel from North Carolina to Tennessee, which direction are you traveling?
    - Ⓐ North
    - Ⓑ South
    - Ⓒ East
    - Ⓓ West

LESSON 10 QUIZ (Lessons 91-100)

...ade in the correct answer.

LANGUAGE ARTS

...laughed when winnie the pooh got stuck in the window
- Ⓐ I laughed when Winnie the Pooh got stuck in the window
- Ⓑ i laughed when winnie the pooh got stuck in the window.
- Ⓒ I laughed when Winnie the Pooh got stuck in the window.
- Ⓓ I laughed when Winnie the Pooh stuck the window.

...are you using youre best handwriting
- Ⓐ Are you using youre best handwriting.
- Ⓑ Are you using your best handwriting?
- Ⓒ Are you using your best handwriting!
- Ⓓ Correct as is

...does you like chocolate and vanilla better
- Ⓐ Does you like chocolate or vanilla better?
- Ⓑ Do you like chocolate or vanilla better?
- Ⓒ Do you like chocolate or vanilla better!
- Ⓓ Does he like chocolate or vanilla better?

SCIENCE

7. What is not one part of the water cycle?
   - Ⓐ Condensation
   - Ⓑ Evaporation
   - Ⓒ Anticipation
   - Ⓓ Precipitation

8. If a sound is caused by a vibration, and the vibration stops, does the sound stop?
   - Ⓐ Yes
   - Ⓑ No

9. What kind of rocks are caused by changes from pressure, heat, liquid, or gas?
   - Ⓐ Igneous rocks
   - Ⓑ Metamorphic Rocks
   - Ⓒ Sedimentary Rocks
   - Ⓓ None of the above

MATH

...A square has how many equal sides?
- Ⓐ 2
- Ⓑ 3
- Ⓒ 4
- Ⓓ 5

...There were 2 pieces of pizza. Josh ate 1 of them. What fraction of the pizza did Josh eat?
- Ⓐ 1/4
- Ⓑ 1/2
- Ⓒ 3/4
- Ⓓ 1 whole

...What number is the Roman numeral IV?
- Ⓐ 3
- Ⓑ 4
- Ⓒ 5
- Ⓓ 6

GEOGRAPHY

10. Which country has these places: Peace River, Winnipeg, and Toronto?
    - Ⓐ United States
    - Ⓑ China
    - Ⓒ India
    - Ⓓ Canada

11. What is Bolivia?
    - Ⓐ A country
    - Ⓑ A continent
    - Ⓒ A pond
    - Ⓓ A state

12. What do you call more than one mountain together?
    - Ⓐ A mountain range
    - Ⓑ A shelf
    - Ⓒ Grasslands
    - Ⓓ None of the above

LESSON 11 QUIZ (Lessons 101-110)

Shade in the correct answer.

LANGUAGE ARTS

1. bill peet writed a lot of good books
   - Ⓐ Bill Peet Wrote a lot of good books.
   - Ⓑ Bill peet wrote a lot of good books.
   - Ⓒ Bill Peet wrote a lot of good books.
   - Ⓓ Correct as is

2. today is the fist day of february
   - Ⓐ Today is the first day of February.
   - Ⓑ Today, the first day of February, it is.
   - Ⓒ Is the first day of February today.
   - Ⓓ Correct as is

3. me and josh got cs on our test
   - Ⓐ Josh and I got cs on our test
   - Ⓑ Me and Josh got Cs on our test.
   - Ⓒ Josh and I got Cs on our test.
   - Ⓓ Correct as is

MATH

4. Count by 6s from 0 to 24.
   - Ⓐ 0, 3, 6, 9, 12, 15, 18, 21, 24
   - Ⓑ 0, 6, 9, 12, 15, 18, 21, 23
   - Ⓒ 0, 6, 12, 18, 24
   - Ⓓ 0, 6, 18, 24

5. What is NOT a fact family for 8, 7, and 15?
   - Ⓐ 15 − 8 = 7
   - Ⓑ 8 + 7 = 15
   - Ⓒ 15 − 7 = 8
   - Ⓓ 8 + 8 = 16

6. How many weeks are in one year?
   - Ⓐ 48 weeks
   - Ⓑ 52 weeks
   - Ⓒ 58 weeks
   - Ⓓ 64 weeks

SCIENCE

7. Which zone of the ocean is closest to the surface?
   - Ⓐ Sunlight zone
   - Ⓑ Twilight zone
   - Ⓒ Midnight zone
   - Ⓓ None of the above

8. If I am using my sense of smell, what part of my body am I using?
   - Ⓐ Ears
   - Ⓑ Fingers
   - Ⓒ Nose
   - Ⓓ Eyes

9. What is at the center of our solar system?
   - Ⓐ Pluto
   - Ⓑ Earth's moon
   - Ⓒ The sun
   - Ⓓ A rocket

GEOGRAPHY

10. What is NOT a state on the West Coast of America?
    - Ⓐ Texas
    - Ⓑ California
    - Ⓒ Oregon
    - Ⓓ Washington

11. What state has the abbreviation NC?
    - Ⓐ North Dakota
    - Ⓑ North Carolina
    - Ⓒ New Mexico
    - Ⓓ New Hampshire

12. Lakes were created by glaciers.
    - Ⓐ True
    - Ⓑ False

LESSON 12 QUIZ (Lessons 111-120)

ade in the correct answer.

LANGUAGE ARTS

wish my dog could talk she would say funny things
- Ⓐ I wish my dog could talk. She would say fun things
- Ⓑ I wish my dog could talk and say funny things.
- Ⓒ I wish my dog could talk, walk, and say funny things.
- Ⓓ I wish my dog could talk. She would say funny things.

what happened to your sisters slipper
- Ⓐ What happened to your sister's slipper.
- Ⓑ What happened to your sister's slipper?
- Ⓒ Where did your sister's slipper go?
- Ⓓ Your sister's slipper is what happened.

valentines day is a fun day for friends
- Ⓐ Valentine's Day is a fun day for friends.
- Ⓑ Valentine's day is a fun day for friends
- Ⓒ Friends like Valentine's Day.
- Ⓓ Correct as is

MATH

What would I use to measure liquids?
- Ⓐ Meter
- Ⓑ Inch
- Ⓒ Yard
- Ⓓ Liter

What number has seven hundreds, nine tens, and five ones?
- Ⓐ 957
- Ⓑ 597
- Ⓒ 7,095
- Ⓓ 795

You made one 2-point basket and one 3-point basket. How many baskets did you score for your team?
- Ⓐ 2 points
- Ⓑ 4 points
- Ⓒ 5 points
- Ⓓ 6 points

SCIENCE

7. An insect's skeleton is on the outside of its body.
   - Ⓐ True
   - Ⓑ False

8. Plants use the air we breathe out.
   - Ⓐ True
   - Ⓑ False

9. What kind of eater was the dinosaur Brachiosaurus?
   - Ⓐ Herbivore (eats plants)
   - Ⓑ Carnivore (eats meat)
   - Ⓒ Omnivore (eats both plants and meat)
   - Ⓓ None of the above

GEOGRAPHY

10. Name the ocean near the East Coast of America.
    - Ⓐ Indian Ocean
    - Ⓑ Pacific Ocean
    - Ⓒ Atlantic Ocean
    - Ⓓ Arctic Ocean

11. What continent does Argentina belong to?
    - Ⓐ South America
    - Ⓑ Asia
    - Ⓒ Europe
    - Ⓓ North America

12. What state has Lake Okeechobee?
    - Ⓐ Arkansas
    - Ⓑ Florida
    - Ⓒ Kansas
    - Ⓓ Michigan

ANSWER KEY

LESSON 1 QUIZ, PAGE 124
1. C
2. B
3. D
4. B
5. A
6. C
7. D
8. B
9. D
10. B
11. A
12. A

LESSON 2 QUIZ, PAGE 125
1. B
2. B
3. C
4. A
5. A
6. C
7. C
8. A
9. A
10. A
11. A
12. D

LESSON 3 QUIZ, PAGE 126
1. D
2. A
3. C
4. B
5. B
6. B
7. A
8. C
9. C
10. D
11. A
12. D

LESSON 4 QUIZ, PAGE 127
1. A
2. D
3. A
4. B
5. B
6. D
7. C
8. B
9. A
10. B
11. C
12. B

LESSON 5 QUIZ, PAGE 128
1. B
2. B
3. D
4. C
5. A
6. B
7. B
8. A
9. A
10. C
11. C
12. A

LESSON 6 QUIZ, PAGE 129
1. C
2. C
3. B
4. A
5. B
6. A
7. D
8. A
9. D
10. D
11. A
12. B

LESSON 7 QUIZ, PAGE 130
1. A
2. D
3. C
4. A
5. C
6. D
7. B
8. A
9. D
10. B
11. D
12. B

LESSON 8 QUIZ, PAGE 131
1. B
2. D
3. D
4. C
5. D
6. B
7. A
8. C
9. C
10. C
11. D
12. B

LESSON 9 QUIZ, PAGE 132
1. A
2. C
3. A
4. D
5. B
6. C
7. A
8. B
9. B
10. C
11. D
12. D

LESSON 10 QUIZ, PAGE 133
1. C
2. B
3. B
4. C
5. B
6. B
7. C
8. A
9. B
10. D
11. A
12. A

LESSON 11 QUIZ, PAGE 134
1. C
2. A
3. C
4. C
5. D
6. B
7. A
8. C
9. C
10. A
11. B
12. A

LESSON 12 QUIZ, PAGE 135
1. D
2. B
3. A
4. D
5. D
6. C
7. A
8. A
9. A
10. C
11. A
12. B